# DANGEROUS RELATIONSHIPS

# OTHER BOOKS BY THE AUTHOR

---

*Behind Closed Doors in White South Africa: Incest Survivors Tell Their Stories*

*Incestuous Abuse: Its Long-Term Effects*

*Against Pornography: The Evidence of Harm*

*Making Violence Sexy: Feminist Views on Pornography*

*Femicide: The Politics of Woman Killing* (with Jill Radford)

*Rape in Marriage*

*Lives of Courage: Women for a New South Africa*

*Exposing Nuclear Phallacies*

*The Secret Trauma: Incest in the Lives of Girls and Women*

*Sexual Exploitation: Rape, Child Sexual Abuse, and Workplace Harassment*

*Against Sadomasochism: A Radical Feminist Analysis* (with Ruth Linden, Darlene Pagano, and Susan Leigh Star)

*Crimes Against Women: The Proceedings of the International Tribunal* (with Nicole Van de Ven)

*The Politics of Rape*

*Rebellion, Revolution and Armed Force*

# DANGEROUS RELATIONSHIPS

## PORNOGRAPHY, MISOGYNY, AND RAPE

DIANA E. H. RUSSELL

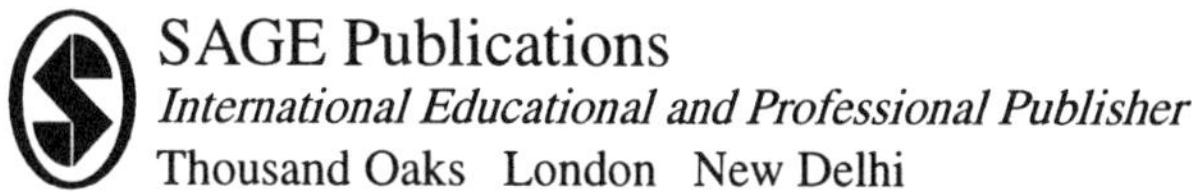

SAGE Publications
*International Educational and Professional Publisher*
Thousand Oaks London New Delhi

---

*For information:*

SAGE Publications, Inc.
2455 Teller Road
Thousand Oaks, California 91320
E-mail: order@sagepub.com

SAGE Publications Ltd.
6 Bonhill Street
London EC2A 4PU
United Kingdom

SAGE Publications India Pvt. Ltd.
M-32 Market
Greater Kailash I
New Delhi 110 048 India

Printed in the United States of America

*Library of Congress Cataloging-in-Publication Data*

Russell, Diane E. H.
Dangerous relationships : pornography, misogyny, and rape / by Diane E.H. Russell.
p. cm.
Includes bibliographical references and index.
ISBN 0761905243 (cloth : acid-free paper)
ISBN 0761905251 (pbk. : acid-free paper)
1. Pornography. 2. Misogyny. 3. Rapists—Psychology. 4. Rape. I. Title.
HQ471 .R933 1998
363.4′7—ddc21 98-8897

This book is printed on acid-free paper.

98 99 00 01 02 03 10 9 8 7 6 5 4 3 2 1

# DEDICATION

*To all feminists who recognize that pornography is a vicious manifestation of misogyny designed to keep women subordinate to men, and who are committed to the fight for a pornography-free world*

## IMPORTANT NOTE:

*Dangerous Relationships: Pornography, Misogyny, and Rape* is a revised and expanded version of my 1994 self-published book, *Against Pornography: The Evidence of Harm.* While the latter volume includes over 100 pornographic pictures, *Dangerous Relationships* merely *describes* these pictures. Several other sections of *Against Pornography* have also been extended in *Dangerous Relationships.*

### How to Order *Against Pornography: The Evidence of Harm*

*Against Pornography* is available or orderable from bookstores as well as from Russell Publications, P.O. Box 118, Shattuck Avenue, Berkeley, CA 94704, U.S.A., $12.95 paperback. For orders from Russell Publications, add $3.00 for postage and handling; California residents please add sales tax.

# CONTENTS

## Part II. Pornographic Pictures as Woman Hatred



## Part III. Pornography as a Cause of Rape

## Part IV. Conclusion

# LIST OF TABLES AND FIGURES

# PREFACE

I have come to dislike talking about the effects of pornography with people who have not seen it for themselves, or whose exposure to it has been so minimal that they equate it with pictures of nude people in sexual encounters. Many women who have seen pornography and who find it upsetting try to discount their distress with a "boys will be boys" shrug. It is no wonder that discussions on this controversial topic frequently descend into verbal combat completely removed from the reality of the degrading portrayals of women featured in pornography.

However, many women become convinced about the harmful effects of pornography after seeing visual examples of this material. I therefore decided to prepare a book manuscript that would include more than 100 examples of pictorial pornography, together with a summary of some of the key scientific research on the impact of pornography on men's rape-related attitudes and behavior. However, because I was unwilling to request the permission of the pornographers who hold the copyrights to reprint these pictures, I was unable to find a publisher who would risk being sued for breach of the copyright laws. (This is not to say that I believe *Against Pornography* does break these laws.[1]) Hence, I decided to publish the illustrated version of this book myself, titling it *Against Pornography: The Evidence of Harm* (Russell, 1994a).

More than 2,000 copies of *Against Pornography* have been sold or given away as of this writing. I have heard from many readers about the powerful impact this book has had on them. In several cases it has completely changed readers' views from a pro-porn or neutral position to a strong anti-porn stance. I have also exposed many audiences in the United States, Canada, Sweden, South

Africa, and the United Kingdom to visual presentations of some of the pornography included in *Against Pornography* along with commentary about each of the pictures.[2] I have witnessed the tremendous effect of this method of educating people about the misogynistic content of pornography.

However, my other commitments have made it impossible for me to spend the time and effort necessary to keep publicizing *Against Pornography*. Hence, I came to realize that I needed to revise this book so that a suitable publisher would be willing to market it without fear of being sued. This would put the publicity and distribution of the book in the hands of professionals. My decision required that I substitute *descriptions* of the pornographic pictures for the actual pictures. I chose the title *Dangerous Relationships: Pornography, Misogyny, and Rape* to convey the book's thesis that there is a significant relationship among pornography, misogyny, and rape that is dangerous to women.

The publication of *Dangerous Relationships* does not, however, herald the demise of *Against Pornography*. I will keep *Against Pornography* in print for readers who believe as I do that it is important for individuals—particularly women—to see the actual pornographic pictures. (For men, it is more often important that they read the *comments* on the pictures; see information on how to order *Against Pornography* on the dedication page). I also believe that it is important for accurate information about pornography to reach a wider audience than the first two printings of *Against Pornography* achieved, so I embarked upon *Dangerous Relationships* with this goal in mind.

Academia continues to be one of the strongholds for pro-pornography advocates and porn fence-sitters—a matter that will be discussed in Part 1. Hence, I am particularly eager to expose the academic community to my theory of pornography as a cause of rape and to bring to their attention the scientific evidence that substantiates this theory. I also want them to become acquainted with a sample of graphic descriptions of the actual content of pornography. Although I first published my causal theory in 1988, it has not yet received the critical attention that I think it deserves. I am hopeful that this will be rectified by the inclusion of *Dangerous Relationships* in Sage Publications' extensive offerings on violence in interpersonal relationships.

As well as substituting descriptions of the pornographic pictures for the pictures themselves, embarking on *Dangerous Relationships: Pornography, Misogyny, and Rape* provided me with the opportunity to revise and expand *Against Pornography*. I have added to the sections on the content of pornography, the circulation rates of the most popular pornographic magazines, the conclusion in Part 4, and the appendixes. The section describing racist pornography has also been moved closer to the beginning. Hence, the numbering systems used for the descriptions of pornographic pictures in *Dangerous Relationships* do not coincide with the numbering of the pictures in *Against Pornography.*

But for four exceptions,[3] I decided to describe the same pictures in *Dangerous Relationships* that I had included in *Against Pornography.* In doing so, I also attempted to correct or complete information that was missing in *Against Pornography* on the sources and dates of the pictures. However, readers will notice that some of the sources of the descriptions of pornographic pictures are still missing. This is because some of the titles of magazines and/or their dates and volume numbers were missing from the porn collections from which I selected the pictures to include.

In my attempts to fill in the missing information on sources, calls to *Penthouse* magazine proved helpful in some instances. A *Hustler* magazine spokesperson, on the other hand, maintained that it would take weeks of labor to locate the publication dates of the visuals I sent to her. The task of completing source information was not made easier by the fact that public libraries rarely house materials that are considered pornographic.

Missing information on the hard-core pornography magazines whose material I wished to include was impossible to trace. Most of these magazines were probably defunct by the 1990s, or appeared under new titles. Indeed, it may well have been impossible to track down most of them even at the time of their publication. Many of the pornographers who publish hard-core magazines operate underground out of fear of prosecution. Some of them deliberately avoid dating their magazines to protect themselves from being sued for illegally using women under 18 years of age.[4] Failure to date a publication also prolongs its apparent currency.

While it would have been easy to select only those pictures that had complete publication information, the dates, sources, and the countries in which they were first published are not important. This information has no relevance to the purpose of this book and of *Against Pornography:* to educate readers about the degradation and abuse of women in pornography.

Although there is considerable overlap between *Against Pornography* and *Dangerous Relationships,* I decided that the extensive revisions justified retitling the work. I also wanted to deter people from assuming that *Against Pornography* is out of print. Keeping the title *Against Pornography* for the revised and expanded book would likely have fostered this assumption. I regret the inconvenience to some readers who may order *Dangerous Relationships* without the opportunity to know the degree to which it overlaps with *Against Pornography.* This confusion will be salient, of course, only for those readers who are already familiar with *Against Pornography.*

## NOTES

1. Stephen Fishman (1996), an attorney and author of an important legal text on copyright law, whom I consulted, expressed the opinion that *Against Pornography* would not violate this law. First, the reprinted pictures are part of a critical scholarly work that was written for educational purposes. Second, the book is not competitive with the publications of the pornographers whose pictures I reprinted. Third, since several of the sources (e.g., *Hustler* and *Playboy*) had policies that would have caused the owners of these magazines to deny me permission to reprint their material had I sought it, I was legally entitled to exercise my right to free speech by disregarding their restrictive rules. The fact that I believed that showing the actual pictures was necessary to effectively communicate my criticism of them and their effects constitutes the rationale for this entitlement.

2. I have always been careful to caution audiences that seeing the pictures may upset them, and I have suggested ways for them to handle this. *Against Pornography* also carries a warning on the cover that reads: "WARNING: some of the visuals in this book may cause distress."

3. I have omitted descriptions and comments on two of the pictures in *Against Pornography,* and I have included descriptions and comments on two additional pictures of Latinas because examples of racist anti-Latina material were missing from this book.

4. Jean Barkey, personal communication to Jan Woodcock, August 26, 1992.

# ACKNOWLEDGMENTS

Jan Woodcock, Ann Simonton, Melissa Farley, and Robert Brannon generously loaned me their pornography collections from which to select the photographs described in this book. Jan provided me with a duplicate set of the slides and accompanying script written by the now defunct Organizing Against Pornography (OAP); as well as some slides from Stopping Violence Against Women (SVAW) in Portland, Oregon; a press release on *Playboy* containing visual pornography prepared by the New York-based Women Against Pornography (WAP); and a handout, also on *Playboy,* compiled by Students Organizing Against Pornography (SOAP). I am greatly indebted to Jan for allowing me to edit and quote from her and OAP's scripts without having to go through the cumbersome practice of repeated acknowledgments. She has also prepared an updated list of feminist anti-pornography organizations currently active in the United States and Canada (see Appendix 3).

I also had at my disposal many slides and an extensive display of visuals from pornographic magazines and newspapers that the former San Francisco-based organization, Women Against Violence in Pornography and Media (WAVPM), had used since its inception in 1976 to educate people about the harms of pornography. I am grateful to all these organizations for their contributions, intended and unintended, to this project. My comments about the pornographic pictures are the result of a collaborative effort.

Several people assisted with the metamorphosis of my article on pornography as a cause of rape, some of which is presented in the introduction to this book, but most of which appears in Part 3. I would particularly like to thank Dorchen Leidholdt, who read a draft of the original article and encouraged me to publish it. She, as well as Catharine MacKinnon and Helen Longino, made some useful suggestions for revisions, and Catharine MacKinnon and Catherine Itzin were very encouraging about its value. Robert Brannon also contributed greatly to my definition of pornography and my discussion of it.

I want to thank Mary Armour and Lisa Koshkarian for writing first drafts of many of the descriptions of the pornographic pictures for *Dangerous Relationships,* and Gayle Pitman and Jackie Thomason for their invaluable editorial assistance. Cath Penavaria also helped by locating the sources for a few of the pornographic pictures described and commented on. I am especially grateful to Roberta Harmes for her remarkable resourcefulness in tracking down books, articles, tables, statistics, obscure references, and other facts and figures, as well as exploring the permissions policies of *Playboy, Hustler,* and *Penthouse* magazines. She was particularly helpful with accessing information on the Internet and providing me with whatever I wanted at a moment's notice. All researchers should be so lucky as to have someone like Roberta to assist them.

I am grateful for the encouragement I have received from many people for undertaking this project, especially Robert Brannon, Jane Caputi, Nikki Craft, Lisa Koshkarian, Anne Mayne, and Ann Simonton.

Last, but not least, I want to thank Peter Labella, my editor at Sage Publications, who was receptive to my proposal that Sage publish this revision of *Against Pornography*. I pointed out to him that Sage's large collection of books on interpersonal violence includes only one book specifically on pornography, a serious oversight that my book would help to rectify. He granted my point and, after consulting the appropriate people at Sage, signed me on.

# PART I

## INTRODUCTION: WHAT IS PORNOGRAPHY?

# DEFINING PORNOGRAPHY

Proponents of the anti-pornography-equals-censorship school deliberately obfuscate any distinction between erotica and pornography, using the term *erotica* for all sexually explicit materials (e.g., Pally, 1994; Strossen, 1995). In contrast, most anti-pornography feminists consider it vitally important to distinguish between pornography and erotica (see Itzin, 1992; Lederer, 1980; Russell, 1993b). While condemning pornography, most of us approve of, or even advocate, erotica.

Although women's bodies are the staple of adult pornography, it is important to have a gender-neutral definition that encompasses the various types of pornography, including gay pornography and child pornography. Animals are also targets of pornographic depictions. Hence, I define *pornography* as *material that combines sex and/or the exposure of genitals with abuse or degradation in a manner that appears to endorse, condone, or encourage such behavior.*[1] However, this book will exclude gay and child pornography, and focus on pornography that abuses or degrades women.

*Erotica* refers to *sexually suggestive or arousing material that is free of sexism, racism, and homophobia and is respectful of all human beings and animals portrayed.* This definition acknowledges the fact that humans are not the only subject matter of erotica. For example, a scene in a documentary on insects titled *Microcosmos,* in which two snails "make love," was highly sensual and erotic.[2] I remember seeing a short award-winning erotic film depicting the peeling of an orange. The shapes and coloring of flowers or hills can make them appear erotic. Many people find Georgia O'Keeffe's paintings erotic. However, erotica can also include overtly or explicitly sexual images.

Canadian psychologists Charlene Senn and Lorraine Radtke (1986) conducted an experiment using slides that demonstrate the significance and meaningfulness to female subjects of distinguishing between pornography and erotica. First, these researchers categorized the slides into three groups:

- violent pornography
- nonviolent but dehumanizing pornography
- erotica (material that was nonsexist and nonviolent)

Then they administered tests of the mood states of their subjects in response to these three categories of slides. They found that both the violent and the nonviolent dehumanizing slides had a negative effect on the mood states of the women subjects, whereas the erotic images had a positive effect (Senn & Radtke, 1986, pp. 15-16; also see Senn, 1993). Furthermore, the violent pornographic pictures had a greater negative impact on the women than did the nonviolent dehumanizing pictures.[3] This shows that a conceptual distinction between pornography and erotica is both meaningful and operational. Experiments conducted by psychologist James Check replicate this finding (Check & Guloien, 1989).

My definition's requirement that erotica must be nonsexist means that the following types of pictorial materials qualify as pornography:

- Sexually arousing images in which women are consistently shown naked while men are clothed
- Pictures in which women's genitals are displayed but men's are not
- Images in which men are always portrayed in the initiating, dominant role

Racist pornography that focuses on people of color typically combines racism and sexism. Yet racism is also manifested in depictions of white women who embody many white males' narrow concept of beauty (very thin, large-breasted, and blonde), since the obvious inference is that women of color don't qualify as sufficiently attractive or beautiful. This form of sexualized racism pervades pornography.

The term *abusive* sexual behavior in my definition of pornography refers to sexual conduct that ranges from derogatory, demeaning, contemptuous, or damaging to that which is brutal, cruel, exploitative, painful, or violent. *Degrading* sexual behavior refers to sexual conduct that is humiliating, insulting, and/or disrespectful: Examples of degrading sexual behavior include urinating or defecating on a woman, ejaculating in her face, treating her as sexually dirty or inferior, depicting her as slavishly following men's orders and eager to engage in whatever sex acts males want, and/or calling her insulting names such as "bitch," "cunt," "nigger," "whore," while engaging in sex.

Feminist philosopher Helen Longino (1980) describes typically abusive and degrading portrayals of female sexuality in many pornographic books, magazines, and films, as follows:

> Women are represented as passive and as slavishly dependent upon men. The role of female characters is limited to the provision of sexual services to men. To the

> extent that women's sexual pleasure is represented at all, it is subordinated to that of men and is never an end in itself as is the sexual pleasure of men. What pleases women is the use of their bodies to satisfy male desires. While the sexual objectification of women is common to all pornography, women are the recipients of even worse treatment in violent pornography, in which women characters are killed, tortured, gang-raped, mutilated, bound, and otherwise abused, as a means of providing sexual stimulation or pleasure to the male characters. (p. 42)

What is objectionable about pornography, then, is its abusive and degrading portrayal of females and female sexuality, not its sexual content or explicitness.

A particularly important feature of my definition of pornography is the requirement that *it appears to endorse,*[4] *condone, or encourage abusive sexual desires or behaviors.* These attributes differentiate pornography from materials that include such abusive or degrading sexual behavior for educational purposes. Movies such as *The Accused* and *The Rape of Love,* for example, are not pornographic because they present realistic representations of rape with the apparent intention of helping viewers to understand the reprehensible nature of rape, as well as the agony experienced by rape victims.

My definition of pornography differs from the current legal definition, which focuses instead on material that is judged to be obscene. It also differs from the definition that I used in previous publications, which limited pornography to sexually explicit materials (e.g., Russell, 1988). I decided to broaden my definition to include materials like slasher films, record covers, and cartoons that meet my definition. In doing so, I am returning to the conception of pornography that we formulated in Women Against Violence in Pornography and Media (WAVPM), the first feminist anti-pornography organization in the United States (see Lederer, 1983).

Some other feminists, however, have included sexual explicitness as a defining feature of pornography. Andrea Dworkin and Catharine MacKinnon (1988), for example, define pornography as "the graphic sexually explicit subordination of women through pictures and/or words" (p. 36). They go on to spell out nine ways in which this overall definition can be met, for example, when "(i) women are presented dehumanized as sexual objects, things, or commodities" (p. 36). Unfortunately, Dworkin and MacKinnon's definition fails to distinguish between materials that depict women as dehumanized sex objects for educational purposes (like the movie *The Accused*—which I consider nonpornographic) and materials that degrade women for males' sexual entertainment and/or sexual gratification.

James Check often uses the term *sexually explicit materials* instead of pornography, presumably in the hope of bypassing the many controversies associated with the term *pornography* (Check & Guloien, 1989, p. 159). However, these scholars have not, to my knowledge, defined what they mean by sexually explicit materials. Because I am unclear about what sex acts qualify as sexually explicit, it is impossible to evaluate the advisability of using this term in my definition.

Some people may object that feminist definitions of pornography that go beyond sexually explicit materials differ so substantially from common usage that they make discussion between feminists and nonfeminists confusing.[5] I would argue, however, that there is no consensus on definitions among either of these groups. Sometimes there is a good reason for feminists to employ the same definition as nonfeminists. For example, in my study of the prevalence of rape, I used a very narrow, legal definition of rape because I wanted to be able to compare the rape rates obtained in my study with those obtained in government studies (see Russell, 1984). Had I used a broader definition that included oral and anal penetration, for example, my study could not have been used to show how grossly flawed the methodology of the government's national surveys is in determining meaningful rape rates. If, however, there is no compelling reason to use a definition with which one disagrees, then it makes sense for feminists to define phenomena in ways that best fit feminist principles.

Unlike Andrea Dworkin and Catharine MacKinnon, most feminists have not attempted to create a definition that would meet legal standards. They devised a definition which, if implemented, would enable someone who has been coerced into pornography, assaulted because of it, or subordinated by trafficking in it, to attempt to prove in a court of law that pornography harmed her (1988, p. 36). More specifically, they defined (and continue to define) pornography as "the graphic sexually explicit subordination of women through pictures and/or words" that also includes one or more of nine conditions, including the following three examples:

> (i) women are presented dehumanized as sexual objects, things, or commodities; . . . or (vi) women's body parts—including but not limited to vaginas, breasts, or buttocks—are exhibited such that women are reduced to those parts; . . . or (ix) women are presented in scenarios of degradation, injury, torture, shown as filthy or inferior, bleeding, bruised, or hurt in a context that makes these conditions sexual.
>
> The use of men, children, or transsexuals in the place of women in [the paragraph] above is also pornography.

Unfortunately, the nine conditions formulated by Dworkin and MacKinnon are typically overlooked by those intent on simplifying it.

Returning to my more concise definition, it should be noted that it does not include all the features that commonly characterize such material. For example, even though pornography frequently depicts female desires and sexuality inaccurately,[6] I have not included this feature of pornography in my definition. It has been shown, for example, that pornography consumers are more likely to believe that unusual sexual practices are more common than they really are (Zillmann & Bryant, 1989). This is hardly surprising in view of the many distortions about female sexuality that pornography typically contains.[7]

*Sexual objectification* is another common characteristic of pornography that I have not included in my definition. It refers to *the portrayal of human beings—usually women—as depersonalized sexual things, such as "tits, cunt, and ass," not as multifaceted human beings deserving equal rights with men.* As Susan Brownmiller (1975) so eloquently noted,

> [In pornography] our bodies are being stripped, exposed and contorted for the purpose of ridicule to bolster that "masculine esteem" which gets its kick and sense of power from viewing females as anonymous, panting playthings, adult toys, dehumanized objects to be used, abused, broken and discarded. (p. 394)

However, the sexual objectification of females is not confined to pornography. It is also a staple of mainstream movies, ads, record covers, songs, magazines, television programs, art, cartoons, literature, and so on, and influences the way that many males learn to see women and even children. This is why I have not included sexual objectification as a defining feature of pornography.

## INCONSISTENCIES IN DEFINITIONS

Many people have commented on the difficulty of defining pornography and erotica, declaring that "one person's erotica is another person's pornography." This statement is often used to deride an anti-pornography stance, as if the lack of consensus on a definition of pornography means that its effects cannot be examined.

However, there is no consensus on the definitions of many phenomena that we nonetheless are willing to take a stand on. Rape is one example. Legal definitions of rape vary considerably in different states. The police often have their own definitions, which may differ from legal definitions. If a woman is raped by someone she knows, for example, the police often "unfound"[8] the case because they are skeptical about many acquaintance and date rapes. Hence, such crimes are rarely investigated. This practice certainly has no basis in the law.

If rape is defined as forced intercourse or attempts at forced intercourse, the problem of figuring out what exactly constitutes force remains. How does one measure it? What is the definition of intercourse? Does it include oral and anal intercourse, intercourse with a foreign object, or digital penetration, or is it defined only as vaginal penetration by the penis? How much penetration is necessary to qualify as intercourse? How does one determine if an attempt at rape has occurred?

How does one deal with the fact that both the rapist and the rape survivor quite often do not believe that a rape has occurred, even when the incident matches the legal definition of rape? Many rapists, for example, do not consider that forcing intercourse on an unwilling woman qualifies as rape because they think the woman's "no" actually means "yes." Many women think they have not been raped when the perpetrator is their husband or lover, even though the law in most states defines such acts as rape.

Fortunately, few people argue that because rape is so difficult to define and because there is no consensus on the best definition of it, it should therefore not be considered a heinous and illegal act.

Similarly, millions of court cases have revolved around arguments as to whether a killing constitutes murder or manslaughter.[9] No one argues that killing should not be subject to legal sanctions just because it takes a court case to decide this question.

The fact that the lack of consensus on how to define pornography is used to discredit any attempt to impose legal restraints on it, or even to express strong opposition to it, whereas no similar argument is made in response to the lack of consensus on definitions of rape and murder, highlights the ideological motivation behind this reasoning. The validity of this point is further substantiated by the fact that nonconsensus on the definition of pornography did not prove to be an obstacle to making pictorial child pornography illegal.

Hence, it is reasonable to conclude that the fixation of pro-pornography advocates on the difficulty of defining pornography is merely a strategy that they employ in their efforts to derail their opponents by making anti-pornography policies appear futile.

## TYPES OF PORNOGRAPHY

Researchers in the United States tend to emphasize the difference between *violent* and *nonviolent* pornography (e.g., Neil Malamuth, Edward Donnerstein, and Daniel Linz). Canadian psychologists James Check and Ted Guloien noted that these researchers have largely accepted the thesis that nonviolent pornography has "minimal if any antisocial effects" (Check & Guloien, 1989, p. 160). Citing feminists who disagree with this conclusion, Check and Guloien distinguished between three types of sexually explicit materials: violent, nonviolent but dehumanizing, and nonviolent and non-dehumanizing (Check, 1985; Check & Guloien, 1989).

Brief descriptions of the contents of the three 30-minute videotapes Check and Guloien (1989) constructed from sexually explicit scenes in commercially produced pornographic videos or from sex education films (described below) help to give substance to their typology. All three of the videotapes portrayed "sexual acts usually leading up to intercourse between a man and a woman" (p. 163).

- The *sexual violence* videotape primarily depicted rape "as having favorable consequences, usually involving the suggestion that the woman enjoyed the experience" (p. 163).
- The *sexually dehumanizing but nonviolent* videotape depicted "sexual interactions in which the woman was portrayed as hysterically responsive to male sexual demands, was verbally abused, dominated, and degraded, and in general treated as a plaything with no human qualities other than her physical attributes. . . . Again, the woman was usually portrayed as enjoying whatever abuse she experienced" (p. 163).
- The *erotica* videotape "consisted of scenes of mutually consenting, affectionately oriented sexual interactions, without any violent or dehumanizing content" (pp. 163-164).

Check and Guloien reserved the term *pornography* for the sexually violent videotape and the sexually dehumanizing but nonviolent videotape.

After distinguishing among these three kinds of sexual material, Check and Guloien conducted a study in which 436 male subjects were asked to indicate their perceptions and evaluations of the three videos. These researchers reported that

> The sexually violent videos were rated as the least educational, realistic, and affectionate, the most obscene, the most offensive, the most aggressive, and the most degrading. In contrast, the erotica was rated as the most educational, realistic, and affectionate, the least obscene, the least offensive, the least aggressive and the least degrading. As expected, the nonviolent, dehumanizing videos were rated in between the sexually violent and the erotica tapes on most of the variables. (Check & Guloien, 1989, pp. 168-169)

The subjects' ratings confirm the meaningfulness of Check and Guloien's distinctions between violent and nonviolent but dehumanizing pornography and erotica.

There are many other bases for distinguishing different types of pornography. For example:

- Pornography may be categorized according to the sexual orientation of the consumers for whom it is produced: heterosexual, gay male, lesbian, and bisexual pornography.
- Pornography may be categorized according to the gender of the individuals used or portrayed in it: pornography using women, men, transgendered people, and those with both male and female bodies.
- Pornography may be categorized according to the gender of the consumers for whom it is produced, for example, *Playboy* for males and *Playgirl* for females. Significantly, the term "men's magazines" is often used as a synonym for pornographic magazines because males are far and away the predominant consumers.
- Pornography may be categorized according to the age of the individuals used or portrayed in it, for example, adult and child pornography.
- Pornography may be categorized according to the degree of intimacy or the seriousness of the sex acts performed or portrayed in it, that is, soft-core and hard-core pornography. (Zillmann and Bryant [1989] define soft-core pornography as "material that features the simulation of sexual behavior rather than their graphic portrayal" [pp. 150-151].)
- Pornography may be categorized according to the medium in which it appears: for example, pornographic films or videos, printed pornography, pictorial pornography, electronic pornography, pornographic computer games, pornographic art, pornographic advertisements, live pornographic shows, and pornographic telephone messages, more commonly referred to as "phone sex." These categories can be further broken down: For example, printed pornography can be differentiated into pornographic novels, magazines, newspapers, zines, cards, cartoons, jokes, and so on. Pornographic art can be differentiated into pornographic drawings, paintings, sculpture, and photography.
- Pornography may be categorized according to the specialized tastes of consumers, often referred to as different genres in pornography: for example, child pornogra-

phy, racist pornography, anti-Semitic pornography, interracial pornography, ethnic pornography (e.g., Asian, African American, Latin/Hispanic), sadomasochistic pornography, snuff pornography, bestiality pornography, geriatric pornography, amputee pornography, large breast pornography, and pornography involving "water sports," rape, incest, bondage, oral sex, fat women, anal sex, defecation/expulsion, torture, piercing, or group sex.

- Pornography may be categorized according to the social class of the consumers to whom it is geared; for example, *Playboy* and *Penthouse* are designed to appeal to middle-class males, whereas *Hustler* is distinctly working class.

## THE CONTENTS OF PORNOGRAPHY

> I've seen some soft-porn movies, which seem to have the common theme that a great many women would really like to be raped, and after being thus "awakened to sex" will become lascivious nymphomaniacs. That . . . provides a sort of rationale for rape: "they want it, and anyway, it's really doing them a favor." (Male respondent quoted in Hite, 1981, p. 787)

There are a growing number of studies analyzing the contents of pornography. However, because there are so many different forms of it and because much of this material—particularly the more violent, degrading, and illegal pornography—is hidden and difficult to find, none of these studies does justice to the scope, magnitude, and seriousness of the problem. Nevertheless, it is important to be aware of the findings of the major studies that have been conducted. I will attempt to point out the major strengths and weaknesses of some of this research.

### *Don Smith's Study*

In an excellent and pioneering study, Don Smith conducted a content analysis of 428 "adults only" fiction paperbacks published between 1968 and 1974 (but excluding 1971). His sample was limited to books that were readily accessible to the general public in the United States, excluding paperbacks that are usually available only in so-called adult bookstores (Smith, 1976b). Every fifth paperback on the shelves of eight stores in eight communities in five states was subjected to a rigorous analysis.

Following are some of Smith's (1976a, 1976b) major findings with regard to rape and forced sex:

- "Almost one-third of the episodes contain the use of some form of force (physical, mental, blackmail), almost always administered by the male, to encourage the female into an initially unwanted act of sex" (1976b, p. 22).
- One fifth of all the sex episodes involved completed rapes (1976a).
- The number of rapes increased with each year's output of newly published books (1976a).
- Of the sex episodes, 6% involved incestuous rape. The focus in the rape scenes was almost always on the victim's fear and terror, which became transformed by the rape into sexual passion. More than 97% of the rapes portrayed in these books resulted in orgasm for the victims. In three quarters of these rapes, multiple orgasm occurred (1976a).
- "Rarely is there any indication of any particular skill or finesse on the part of the male. Seemingly it is his sheer sexuality and size of his sex organs to which the female responds" (1976b, p. 22).
- "Although bestiality is not a common occurrence in these episodes, in 70 percent of its cases it is in some way forced on the female by the male. Yet again, however sincere her resistance, four-fifths of the time the female physically responds and is immediately consumed by shame and humiliation at her physical satisfaction" (1976b, p. 23).

Not surprisingly, Smith (1976b) notes that the theme of hypermasculinity dominated these books: "These are the acts of virile, red-blooded males, the traditional male stereotype magnified tenfold" (p. 22). Males dominated the sexual encounters "regardless of the kind of sex, the setting, the people, or the numbers involved. . . . Even the episodes of female self-masturbation are male dominated" (p. 22). For example, the male characters often forced the females to engage in self-masturbatory acts. Similarly, in one third of the sexual encounters between women,

> the behavior is either instigated by, or forced on, one or both of the females by the male. A common theme is that a good male is all that is needed to turn even the most committed lesbian to at least bisexuality (and if she doesn't she usually meets with an ill fate in the plot). (Smith, 1976b, p. 22)

Sexism is also evident in the depictions of physical appearance. Smith (1976b) comments that

> Physical characteristics of the female are described in minute detail, down to the last dimple. For more than one-fourth of the male characters, however, nothing is said about their physical features with the exception of almost universal reference to the large size of their genitals. (p. 21)

Smith emphasizes the impersonal nature of the sexual encounters described in these pornographic books. For example, "overt or even implicit expression of love toward the other partner" occurs in only 9% of the sex acts. "Sixty percent of the sex episodes are characterized by . . . sheer physical gratification devoid of any feeling toward the partner as a person" (1976b, p. 22).

Analysis of the characteristics of the 3,108 principal characters in these pornographic books revealed that 98% of the males and 99% of the females were white. In those instances in which people of color were portrayed, they almost always had sexual encounters with whites: "Sexual behavior between non-white males and non-white females is infinitesimal in this literature," Smith (1976b, p. 21) observed. In addition, of the 87% of the principal male characters whose occupations were specified, 55% were portrayed as professional, business, or white-collar compared to only 4% of the females (Smith, 1976b, p. 20). None of the male characters was unemployed or had a blue-collar occupation.

Hence, it is evident that the male characters in these pornographic books enjoyed relatively high status, particularly in comparison with the females, thus increasing the likelihood that they will be seen as positive role models by male consumers.

Smith's content analysis shows that the "adult only" paperbacks that he analyzed are thoroughly permeated by sexism and misogyny. Racism is primarily evident in the virtual absence of all people of color from these books. On the basis of Smith's findings, the common feminist characterization of pornography as woman-hating propaganda is clearly no exaggeration.

### *Neil Malamuth and Barry Spinner's Study*

Neil Malamuth and Barry Spinner (1980) undertook a content analysis to determine the amount of sexual violence in cartoons and pictorials in *Penthouse* and *Playboy* magazines from June 1973 to December 1977. They found that:

- By 1977, about 5% of the pictorials and 10% of the cartoons were sexually violent (p. 235).[10]

- Sexual violence in pictorials (but not in cartoons) increased significantly over the 5-year period, "both in absolute numbers and as a percentage of the total number of pictorials" (p. 226).
- *Penthouse* contained more than twice the percentage of sexually violent cartoons as *Playboy* (13% vs. 6%, respectively; p. 226).

### *Joseph Scott and Steven Cuvelier's Study*

Joseph Scott and Steven Cuvelier undertook a more recent quantitative analysis of violence in *Playboy* magazine from 1953 to 1983 (Scott & Cuvelier, 1987). These researchers reported that the number of "sexually violent portrayals was minimal in comparison to the overall portrayals over this period," and that the amount of this material had decreased over the years (Scott & Cuvelier, 1993, p. 363). Of course, the percentages of sexually violent cartoons and pictorials Malamuth and Spinner found in *Playboy* and *Penthouse* were also very low (5% of the pictorials and 10% of the cartoons). The difference between Malamuth and Spinner (1980) and Scott and Cuvelier is that the former two researchers considered even these small percentages to be cause for concern.

Scott and Cuvelier (1993) reported that Malamuth had provided an explanation for the decrease in sexual violence in *Playboy* that they found between 1953 and 1983. He informed them that *Playboy* owner Hugh Hefner had instructed his editors to avoid violent imagery as a result of Malamuth and Spinner's (1980) research (Smith & Cuvelier, 1993, p. 363, fn. 9). Hence, Scott and Cuvelier decided to conduct a similar content analysis of violent cartoons and pictorials in *Hustler*—which they refer to as a "male sophisticate magazine"—from 1974 to 1987 (1993, p. 363). Sexually violent depictions in *Hustler* magazine "were neither prevalent nor increasing," according to Scott and Cuvelier (1993, p. 369). More specifically, sexually violent cartoons accounted for only 0.36% of the cartoons, and only 0.61% of the pictorials were sexually violent (1993, p. 368).

I am confident that Scott and Cuvelier's figures would be very substantially higher if their study were to be replicated by researchers who are not intent on understating the number of depictions of sexual violence in so-called male sophisticate magazines. Even their choice of this bizarre phrase as a descriptor of pornographic magazines reveals the strength of their bias. So eager are they to underplay the amount of sexual violence in *Hustler* magazine that they make the following ludicrous statement: "violent or sexually violent depictions were identified on 16.7 and 9.7 [respectively] of every 1000 pages of the magazine"

(Scott & Cuvelier, 1993, p. 369). Clearly, it makes no sense to report the number of such depictions as a ratio of total pages, many of which are devoid of pictures!

Scott and Cuvelier's (1993) bias is made explicit in their instructions to the students who did the content analysis. They told the students who evaluated the sexually violent content of *Hustler* magazine that "if the stimulus was ambiguous" they should be conservative and not rate it as sexually violent (p. 364). It appears that the students found a great deal of ambiguous material!

Revealing another example of bizarre and biased terminology, as well as a gross misunderstanding of anti-pornography feminists' thinking, Scott and Cuvelier (1993) contend that

> Today's renewed concern with the effects of pornography originated with the *"conservative feminist"* contention that sexually explicit depictions are degrading to women and responsible for increases in sexual assaults. (p. 358; emphasis mine)

I personally do not know a single feminist who believes that pornography is the singular cause of sexual assaults and therefore the only factor responsible for increases in these crimes. In addition, labeling anti-pornography feminists as conservative renders the term quite meaningless. This label equates anti-pornography feminists with right-wing conservatives—a comparison that is totally erroneous. Since supporters of pornography hate right-wingers because right-wingers typically favor censoring pornography, Scott and Cuvelier's characterization of anti-pornography feminists as conservative is presumably intended to convey that we are also pro-censorship, thereby discrediting our analysis of pornography as well as our fight against it.

### *Joseph Slade's Study*

Joseph Slade (1984) reports that thrice-yearly surveys from 1979 to 1984 based on samples of about 300 pornographic loops or videotapes at the three largest arcades in Times Square show that, "Only in 1981 did levels of violence—coded by the standards used in the Kinsey Institute survey—exceed 11 percent" (p. 162). Slade fails to mention the levels of violence in other years.

With regard to pornographic feature films like *Behind the Green Door* and *Deep Throat,* Slade maintains that

> random viewings of pornographic features over the last four years suggest that violent elements occur in about 16 percent, although relatively mild aggression far outweighs brutality. (p. 162)

Like Scott and Cuvelier, Slade repeatedly notes that most pornographic material is not violent, rather than emphasizing the quantity that *is* violent. Furthermore, all three researchers completely ignore the far larger percentage of *dehumanizing* pornography. Their analysis downplays the significance of violent and degrading material. This is as inappropriate as it would be if a hypothetical criminologist were to report that only, say, 10% of all crimes are violent. Use of the word *only* minimizes the fact that 10% represents a large number of individuals, many of whom will suffer greatly as a result of these crimes of violence.

### *T. S. Palys's Study*

In a content analysis of a sample of 150 sexually-oriented home videos in Vancouver, Canada, T. S. Palys (1986) found that 19% of all the scenes involved aggression, and 13% involved sexual aggression (pp. 26-27). Of all the sexually aggressive scenes in the "adult" videos, 46% involved bondage or confinement; 23%, slapping, hitting, spanking, or pulling hair; 22%, rape; 18%, sexual harassment; 4%, sadomasochism; and 3%, sexual mutilation. In comparison, 38% of all the sexually aggressive scenes in the triple-X videos involved bondage or confinement; 33%, slapping, hitting, spanking, or pulling hair; 31%, rape; 17%, sexual harassment; 14%, sadomasochism; and 3%, sexual mutilation (p. 31).

While Palys's analysis focuses largely on the unexpected finding that "adult" videos "have a significantly greater absolute number of depictions of sexual aggression per movie than triple-X videos," the more relevant point is that violence against women in both types of pornographic videos is quite common, and that rape is one of the more prevalent forms of sexual violence depicted. I would expect a comparable content analysis of videos in the United States to reveal more rape and other sexual violence than was found in this Canadian study because the Canadian government has played a more active role than the U.S. government in trying to restrict the most abusive categories of pornography.

Palys (1986) did not find an increase in the amount of sexual violence portrayed in these videos over time. However, as he points out, it was not clear whether this was because some proprietors had become sensitized to issues of sexual violence as a result of protests by Canadian women, or whether they hoped to avoid protests by selecting less violent fare in recent years (p. 34).

### *Park Elliott Dietz and Alan Sears's Study*[11]

An extensive analysis of the contents of the covers of pornographic books, magazines, and "the front packaging material for videotape cassettes or films" (hereafter referred to as videotape covers) was directed by Park Elliott Dietz, a forensic psychiatrist and former Commissioner on the Attorney General's Commission on Pornography, and Alan Sears, the former Executive Director of this Commission (1987/1988, pp. 12-13). The data were collected from randomly selected pornography outlets in four major U.S. cities—Washington, D.C., New York, Baltimore, and Boston—by Commission staff between October 1985 and May 1986, and analyzed by Dietz and Sears after the Commission had disbanded.

Dietz and Sears (1987/1988) argue that their focus on covers underplayed the degrading nature of the pornography. They note, for example, that "of the 105 works examined internally after the cover imagery had been classified, all but two contained imagery that was more sexually explicit or deviant than the cover" (p. 13). Furthermore, these researchers analyzed only material that was openly displayed. It is well known that more extreme pornography is often kept "under the counter" for trusted customers at such stores.

A selection of Dietz and Sears's major findings is quoted in the following numbered paragraphs. A critique of these researchers' findings and the categories they devised will be provided at the end of this description of their content analysis. It is important to be aware that each cover could contribute to more than one of the content descriptions.

3. Approximately 3% of the items depicted the use of force (rape, whipping, spanking, and women fighting).
4. Approximately 1% of the items depicted the effects of violence (bruising, blood, and some instances of piercing and corpses).
5. Approximately 5% of the items depicted implements of violence (other than simple restraints), whether in use or not (whips, guns, knives, or other weapons; hoists or racks).
6. Approximately 10% of all items depicted sexual bondage (gags, blindfolds, hoods, or masks worn by persons in dominant or submissive

positions, neck restraints, handcuffs, leg irons, or other restraint of the body).

7. Approximately 12% of all items depicted sadomasochistic imagery (sexual bondage, forcible rape, the sexual use of piercing, whipping, or weapons, or sexual depictions of bruising or blood).
8. Approximately 13% of all items depicted violence (bondage, sadism evidenced other than by bondage, spanking, women fighting, or fisting[12]).
9. Approximately 10 to 15% of all items depicted imagery corresponding to the particular interests of paraphiles (excluding sadomasochistic imagery), including: corpses (corresponding to necrophilia); enemas (corresponding to klismaphilia); urine or urination (corresponding to urophilia); feces or defecation (corresponding to coprophilia); diapers or diapering (corresponding to infantilism); bestiality (corresponding to zoophilia); anatomically normal men wearing female clothing (corresponding to transvestic fetishism); leather, rubber, latex, or exaggerated shoes and boots (corresponding to fetishism); and childlike clothing, props, or settings and shaved pubic hair (corresponding to hebophilia and less successfully to pedophilia).
10. No pornographic photographs of prepubescent children were observed, but twelve of thirteen outlets sold books on child sexual abuse and incest that contained detailed and sexually explicit written descriptions of sexual activity between children and adults.
11. The 13% of materials depicting imagery corresponding to the particular interests of sexual sadists and sexual masochists overlap somewhat with the 10 to 15% of materials corresponding to other paraphilic interests. The best estimate that can be made of the proportion of all materials designed to correspond to paraphilic interests is one quarter of all materials.
13. Approximately 11% of all items depicted group sexual activity.
14. Approximately 10% of all items focused on particular body states (partial transsexuals,[13] extremely large breasts, pregnancy, or engorged breasts with milk production).
15. The proportions of all items depicting particular sexual acts were: fellatio (22%), anal insertion of the penis (12%), vaginal intercourse (7%), cunnilingus (7%), masturbation (4%), and penetration by inanimate objects (3%).
16. The 7% of materials depicting vaginal intercourse include materials showing group sex or various deviant sexual activities in association with vaginal intercourse. Less than 5% of all merchandise depicted vaginal intercourse between only one man and one woman.
18. Less than 10% of the materials depict normal heterosexual activities between a man and a woman, and less than half of these depict vaginal intercourse. (Dietz & Sears, 1987/1988, pp. 38-40)

These findings prompted Dietz and Sears to observe that

> there may be a genre of pornography that depicts couples "making love," but if there is, it occupies little or no shelf space in the "adults-only" bookstores of America. (p. 10)

Dietz and Sears conclude their content analysis with the following statement:

> Assuming that sexual violence, sexual degradation, and sexual humiliation are everywhere regarded as unwholesome and unhealthy, we conclude that a large proportion of the current "adults-only" pornography market consists of unwholesome and unhealthy merchandise according to any reasonable standard. (pp. 38-40)

*Evaluation of the Dietz-Sears Study.* While the Dietz and Sears study is arguably the most comprehensive and well-substantiated content analysis of pornography to date outside of cyberspace (see Marty Rimm's [1995] more comprehensive content analysis of pornography on the Internet), it suffers from some profound limitations. Aside from confining their investigation to the covers of books, magazines, and videotapes, and the unrepresentativeness of the pornography outlets and cities included in their study, Dietz and Sears fail to make gender a focal point of their analysis and discussion.

For example, Dietz and Sears's conclusion that most pornography is "unhealthy" ignores the point that it is mostly women who are victimized by men in pornography. In cases where this is not so, it is because the pornography is geared to male masochists or to the gay male or lesbian markets. The point is that the industry is primarily focused on appealing to male customers, and most of these customers want to see men dominating, being serviced by, and/or hurting women. Merely to report the percentages of pictures in which violence is depicted distorts an intrinsic feature of heterosexual pornography: that it is almost exclusively women who are subject to this violence. But since Dietz and Sears's study is not limited to heterosexual pornography, one cannot extrapolate from it the percentages in which women are the targets of the violence.

In the Dietz and Sears study, violent or abusive acts of major concern to feminists seem to be missing or transmuted into something else. Depictions of rape are incorporated into the sadomasochistic category (Dietz & Sears, 1987/1988, p. 25). There are no categories for depictions of beating, kicking, battery, torture, or murder, but there is for "spanking"—a term preferred by sadomasochists because it sounds less serious and more plausibly consensual.

Furthermore, although Dietz and Sears have a content category labeled "child-like clothing, props, or setting" for pictures of "pseudochild pornography" (i.e., pornography that uses adult women posing as children), they appear to have no category for portrayals of incestuous abuse (Dietz & Sears, 1987/1988, p. 28). Nor do they explain this serious omission. Dietz and Sears clearly came across portrayals of incestuous abuse. They note, for example, that "items such as *Kneeling for Daddy, Slave Wife Sucks, Daddy's Hot Daughter,* and *Virgin and the Lover,* are probably not accurate representations of the family relations or chastity of the performers" (p. 15), but they nevertheless omit incestuous abuse from their quantitative analysis. It makes no sense to distinguish between depictions of "Hood or mask worn by person in submissive position" and "Hood or mask worn by person in dominant position" (p. 19), but to fail to distinguish between representations of incestuous abuse and nonfamilial child sexual abuse.

Similarly, Dietz and Sears (1987/1988) mention titles accompanying pictures "indicating themes of racial bigotry against Blacks, Hispanics, or Asians, religious bigotry against Jews or Catholics, and, most commonly, sexual bigotry against women" (p. 15), yet they fail to provide a quantitative analysis of these different forms of bigotry (p. 15). Although they refer the reader to a very long alphabetical listing of ethnic titles in the Final Report of the Attorney General's Commission on Pornography (1986), this is no substitute for quantification. Searching for titles referring to Hispanic women is like looking for a needle in a haystack because there are so few of them and because ethnicity is not always obvious from the titles.

Dietz and Sears appear to consider all depictions that deviate from conventional heterosexual relations to be extra degrading. For example, pictures of "anatomically normal men wearing female clothing" and of people dressed in leather or wearing exaggerated shoes and boots are lumped in with bestiality and sexual depictions of enemas, urine or urination, and feces or defecation (1987/1988, p. 27).

In order to deal with peoples' different attitudes and values regarding sexual behavior, Dietz and Sears (1987/1988) differentiated among three perspectives on what constitutes degrading and humiliating pornography: the sexually traditional, the sexually moderate, and the sexually liberal (p. 40). They define sexual liberals as "those who have by and large accepted the changes in social behavior that accompanied the sexual revolution of the 1960's" (p. 32). Dietz and Sears claim that sexual liberals would consider about 13% of the pornographic material they surveyed to be violent, about 23% to be degrading or humiliating, and about 64% to be nonviolent, nondegrading, and nonhumiliating (p. 40).

Once again, whatever happened to gender? Since when do men and women who have seen a comprehensive sample of pornography have identical views about it? I also disagree with Dietz and Sears's contention that sexual liberals would consider pictures of transvestites, "leather fetish items," exaggerated shoes and boots, and "a person with breasts and a penis" (p. 33) to be degrading. Indeed, I think a lot of sexual liberals would also find some of the bondage images acceptable.

While Dietz and Sears are perfectly cognizant of the fact that pornography victimizes primarily women, this is not reflected in their content coding categories. For example, categories like whipping, piercing, bruising, and spanking do not reveal the gender of the victims and perpetrators of these acts. If it were not for the fact that pornography is so sexist that the gender of perpetrators and victims can reasonably be inferred, the results of Dietz and Sears's content analysis of pornography would be of little interest to feminists.

These criticisms are not intended totally to negate the usefulness of Dietz and Sears's content analysis of pornography. Most research on pornography has been done by men, few of whom have a woman-oriented or feminist perspective. As long as the researchers' biases and distortions do not completely destroy the significance of their work, it is advisable to use what is valuable in it and discard the rest.

### *Feminist Research*

In contrast to Dietz and Sears and most other pornography researchers, Gloria Cowan and Wendy Stock, among others, are guided by a feminist perspective on pornography. Cowan and Stock (1995) are critical of the fact that "most researchers recognize only the distinction between violent and nonviolent pornography" (p. 105; also see Check & Guloien, 1989). Several researchers grant the harmful effects of violent pornography while maintaining or implying that nonviolent material is harmless, including "pornography that is degrading and dehumanizing, but *not* explicitly violent" (Cowan & Stock, 1995, p. 105).

### *Gloria Cowan, Carole Lee, Daniella Levy, and Debra Snyder's Study*

The following excellent content analysis conducted by Gloria Cowan, Carole Lee, Daniella Levy, and Debra Snyder (1988) highlights how vital it is for researchers to include gender analyses when conducting research on pornography.

Cowan, along with Carole Lee, Daniella Levy, and Debra Snyder, selected 45 widely available X-rated videotapes manufactured between 1979 and 1985, including "classics" such as *Deep Throat, Behind the Green Door,* and *Devil in Miss Jones II* (p. 302). They identified 443 sex scenes in these videotapes—about 10 per video. Each of the sex scenes was assigned to one of the following four categories based on its predominant theme (p. 303):

- *Domination:* Scenes depicting "one participant controlling the sex act, either physically or verbally" (pp. 303-304).
- *Exploitation:* Scenes involving "participant(s) clearly using one or more participants without consideration of the used person(s)," and typically including inequality in age, status, occupation, and state of undress (p. 304).
- *Reciprocity:* Scenes involving "mutual consent and mutual satisfaction, including both verbal and nonverbal expression of reciprocity or mutual satisfaction" (p. 304).
- *Autoerotic:* Scenes depicting masturbation or other kinds of self-stimulation.

Cowan and her colleagues (1988) reported that 28% of the sex scenes portrayed dominance, 26% exploitation, 37% reciprocity, and 9% autoeroticism. Not surprisingly, these researchers also observed that, "Men did most of the domination and exploitation" (p. 306). When women were depicted as dominant or exploitive, it was typically with other women. Ninety-five percent of the autoerotic scenes depicted women. When the analysis focused on the entire videotape rather than the sex scene, *just over three quarters (78%) of the videos included themes of dominance, and 82% of the videos portrayed sexual exploitation.*

The content of the sex scenes depicting dominance or exploitation were analyzed for the presence of 13 more specific indicators of dominance and inequality. For example, almost a quarter (23%) of the sex scenes portrayed physical aggression, 20% verbal aggression, 28% verbal dominance, 14% submission, 6% rape, 3% bondage, 3% incest, 39% status inequalities, and 18% verbal inequalities.

Cowan et al. (1988) defined rape as unexpected, unprovoked attacks (presumably, involving forced intercourse) in which the victim remained unwilling throughout; and they used the term *submission* to refer to sexual advances in which one or more resisting participant is induced or coerced into participation "and eventually cooperates and/or enjoys it" (p. 304). Acts of submission are often referred to as "rapes with positive outcomes." Given the popularity of these myth-perpetuating "rapes" in pornography, perhaps *pornographic rape* would be a more appropriate term to use. Clearly, had Cowan and her colleagues combined depictions of rape and pornographic rape, the percentage of videotapes depicting rape would have been substantially higher.

When the focus was shifted from sex scenes to the entire videotape, Cowan et al. (1988) noted that *almost three quarters (73%) of the videos depicted physical aggression, and just over half (51%) depicted rape—not including pornographic rape*. Females were the victims in all the rape scenes, 90% of which portrayed a man raping a woman, and 10% of which portrayed a woman rapist (p. 307).

The 14 scenes depicting incest portrayed "mother-son, sister-sister, brother-sister, aunt-nephew, and uncle-niece incest"; father-daughter incest was not depicted in any of the 45 videos (Cowan et al., 1988, p. 307). Ten of the 14 bondage scenes portrayed female bondage, and 4 portrayed male bondage. When a man was bound, Cowan and colleagues report that it was done playfully and in a mood of reciprocity, whereas "when a female was bound, it was done in a violent, abusive manner and was associated with a mood rating of dominance" (p. 307). This finding, like many of the others, reveals the important revelations that often emerge from gender analyses—particularly in the study of pornography.

With regard to status inequality, Cowan et al. (1988) noted that 62% of the main male characters in the videotapes were professionals or businessmen, whereas "the professions of the women, when identified, were traditional: 58% were clerical/secretarial workers, students, or housewives" (p. 307). These findings are very similar to those reported by Smith (1976a, 1976b) in his analysis of "adult-only" paperbacks. Cowan et al. (1988) also reported that the main male character was usually not completely naked whereas "the woman was almost always naked except for the ever-present garter-belt and high-heels (usually black)" (p. 308). When the woman was depicted as inexperienced, her garter-belt was white. Cowan et al. interpret the more frequent close-up shots of female genitals as compared with male genitals in these videotapes as indicative of the greater objectification of women.

These researchers also observed that kissing was very infrequent and that the upper bodies of the male and female characters in the videos very rarely touched during sexual intercourse.

> The man typically remained in this position until right before ejaculation, at which time he would withdraw his penis and ejaculate on the woman's stomach, face, breasts, or back just above the buttocks. . . . The scene would end with the man ejaculating on the woman a second time, and the woman would either lick it up

> or rub it over her body. In most of these scenes, the man was expressionless and the woman moaned with pleasure. (Cowan et al., 1988, pp. 307-308)

This description conveys the lack of love, affection, tenderness, or mutuality that is typical of pornographic sex, as well as the myth that all women love swallowing semen or having it spurt in their faces or on other regions of their bodies.

Cowan et al. concluded that the 45 widely available made-for-men X-rated videotapes that they analyzed provided a distorted picture of male and female sexuality "that is especially degrading to women" (p. 309). They also noted that "a significant level of hatred of women is now available for viewing in our living rooms and bedrooms" (p. 310).

### *Gloria Cowan and Robin Campbell's Study*

As with gender, an analysis of the relevance of race or ethnicity often reveals important new insights that are lost in race-/ethnicity-blind studies—as is evident in the following study conducted by Cowan and Robin Campbell. To date, racism in pornography has been a relatively neglected topic.

Cowan and Campbell (1994) undertook a content analysis of racism and sexism in interracial sex scenes in 54 X-rated pornography videotapes. Because their findings regarding sexism were consistent with Cowan et al.'s 1988 study, the following summary will focus on some of Cowan and Campbell's (1994) major statistically significant findings regarding racism and its interrelationship with sexism.

- African American women were subjected to "a greater number of different acts of physical and nonphysical aggression than were White women" (p. 335).
- White women were subjected to more acts of physical aggression by African American men, whereas African American women were subjected to more acts of physical aggression by white men (p. 332).
- "Both women and men were significantly more verbally aggressive toward their cross-race partners than toward their same-race partners" (p. 333).
- African American women were more often treated as objects by white men, whereas white women were more often treated as objects by African American men (p. 333). ("Objectification was scored when the character appeared to be less than human or where her/his presence in the scene was as an object or ornament" [p. 329].)

- African American women "performed fellatio on their knees more ⌊ White women. . . . In contrast, White women were ejaculated on the than Black women . . . , especially by White men" (p. 333).
- African American women were more often portrayed than white wome⌊ initially resisting sexual activity but eventually submitting to it (p. 335).
- African American men scored significantly lower on intimacy than white men (p. 334). (The criteria for evaluating intimacy consisted of "kissing, using the other person's name, caressing, having intercourse face to face, and talking during sexual activity" [p. 328].)
- African American men were portrayed as having a larger penis than white men. More specifically, 22% of the African American men had large penises compared to only 4% of the white men (p. 334).

Cowan and Campbell (1994) note that the portrayal of white men as more frequently physically aggressive toward African American women than toward white women is consistent with the white men's treatment of African American women as chattel during slavery in the United States. They also suggest that the cross-race effects they found "may be an expression of interracial hostility in which women are the victims of outrage at interracial sex" (p. 336). In addition, they hypothesize that the greater number of acts of physical aggression by African American men toward white women that emerged from their data analysis may be "a punishment for having sex with a Black man" (p. 336). All three of these hypotheses seem highly plausible.

The popularity in pornography of "rape with positive outcomes," or what I am proposing to call pornographic rape, reveals that many male consumers enjoy the idea of women as animals whose bodies betray them by responding ecstatically to coerced intercourse despite their initial attempts to reject the men's advances. Cowan and Campbell's finding that African American women were portrayed more often than white women as initially resisting sexual activity but eventually surrendering to it reflects the racist stereotype that African American women are more animal-like than white women.

Cowan and Campbell conclude their analysis by maintaining that pornography reinforces racial and sexual stereotypes and that it portrays African American men and women in an even more sexist manner than white men and women. Whereas white women were dominated in pornographic interracial videos, African American women were dominated even more intensely, and whereas white men were portrayed as sex machines, African American men were portrayed as even more impersonal sex machines.

These two illuminating and rigorous studies by Cowan and her colleagues demonstrate the value of utilizing a feminist framework when conducting research on pornography. These researchers do not confine their analysis to measuring violent content. Instead, they focus more broadly on quantifying content that reflects inequality, exploitation, and harm rather than deviance, and they can be relied upon to pay attention to gender and race.

### *In Summary*

Since most of these studies focus on different kinds of pornography ("adult-only" fiction; pornographic videotapes; the covers of pornographic magazines, books, and videotapes; or *Playboy, Penthouse,* and *Hustler* magazines), it is hardly surprising that the analyses of content yield very different results. However, the results are also greatly affected in some cases by methodological problems, including an extreme anti-feminist bias in the case of Scott and Cuvelier (1987, 1993) and a failure to quantify degrading, exploitive, and unequal depictions, and to analyze them in terms of gender and ethnicity. More studies like those of Smith and of Cowan and her colleagues are needed. Nevertheless, it is reasonable to conclude the following:

- While most pornography does not portray explicitly violent acts against women, a very significant quantity of such pornography exists.
- Even nonfeminist research (e.g., Dietz & Sears, 1987/1988) shows that pornography greatly distorts the reality of female sexuality, and contains large quantities of depictions that are degrading and dehumanizing to women. The research by Cowan and her colleagues succeeds in rigorously documenting this conclusion.

The findings on whether or not pornography has become more violent over time are even less conclusive than the studies of content only. Smith's and Malamuth's studies document an increase over time; Palys's study, which found no increase in violence in X-rated videos, was conducted in Canada—a country that has been significantly more restrictive of pornography than the United States; and Scott and Cuvelier's studies claiming no increase in violent content in *Playboy* and *Hustler* are too biased to trust. Clearly, more and better research is needed on this subject.

These studies aside, there are several other studies about the impact of viewing pornography that provide compelling reasons to believe that pornography has become more violent, degrading, and exploitive of women over time. These studies will be described in following sections of this book, and their implications with regard to the increase in misogynist depictions over time will be taken up again in the conclusion of this volume.

## THE CIRCULATION RATES FOR SELECTED PORNOGRAPHIC MAGAZINES

For those of us who believe that pornography is a clear and present danger to women and children, it is important to know how widespread the consumption of pornography is. Because the visual evidence of the harmfulness of pornography presented in Part 2 is confined to the pictures in porn magazines, I will limit my consumption analysis to the circulation rates, as judged by the number of paid subscriptions, for the seven oldest and best-known pornographic magazines in the United States.

The circulation rates for magazines include the number of paid subscriptions and the number of newsstand sales in a 1-year period. In the following analysis, the circulation rates will be confined to those occurring within the United States.

The circulation rates for pornography magazines are obtained by the publishers and are not checked against circulation audit statements (see *The Standard Periodical Directory,* 1997). How correct they are depends therefore on the honesty and accuracy of the individuals responsible for compiling and reporting this information.

An examination of three U.S. magazine directories reveals some very large discrepancies in the subscription rates recorded for some pornography magazines. For example, the 1997 rate for *Hustler* magazine ranged from a low of 500,000 in one directory to a high of 1,426,000 in another (see Appendix 1, Table A.1.1). Similarly, the subscription rate for *Chic* in 1996 ranged from 50,000 to 90,876 (*Working Press of the Nation* [National Research Bureau, 1977] and *Bacon's Magazine Directory* [1977], respectively). Because of these large discrepancies, the subscription rates reported in Table 1.1 are the averages of the rates recorded in these three directories. *The Standard Periodical Directory* (1997) is the source for newsstand sales in Table 1.1 because this information was not provided by the other three directories. This table also specifies the years in which these seven porn magazines were launched.

Table 1.1 omits many porn magazines, some of them offshoots of their better-known parent publications. For example, other *Hustler* publications include *Hustler Busty Beauties, Hustler Erotic Video Guide, Hustler Fantasies,*

**TABLE 1.1** Circulation Rates for Selected U.S. Pornography Magazines in 1997, and Year Established

| *Pornography Magazine* | *Subscription Rates* | *Newsstand Rates*[a] | *Total Circulation* | *Year Established* |
|---|---|---|---|---|
| *Playboy* | 3,451,888 | 642,923 | 4,094,811 | 1953 |
| *Penthouse* | 1,368,236 | 744,836 | 2,113,072 | 1969 |
| *Hustler* | 808,667 | 1,250,000 | 2,058,667 | 1974 |
| *Club* | 700,000 | 756,440 | 1,456,440 | 1975 |
| *Gallery* | 433,333 | 17,791 | 451,124 | 1972 |
| *Oui* | 357,500 | 291,000 | 648,500 | 1972 |
| *Chic* | 95,438 | 130,000 | 225,438 | 1976 |
| **Total:** | 7,215,062 | 3,832,990 | 11,048,052 | |
| Percentage: | 65% | 35% | | |

NOTE: a. With the exception of *Gallery,* the page numbers for newsstand sales in *The Standard Periodical Directory* (1997) were: *Playboy,* p. 1269; *Penthouse,* p. 1786; *Hustler,* p. 1785; *Club,* p. 1267; *Oui,* p. 1786; *Chic,* p. 1784. The number of newsstand sales for *Gallery* was obtained from Endicott (1996, p. S17), because this information was missing from *The Standard Periodical Directory.*

and *Hustler Humor* (*Ulrich's International Periodical Directory, 1996* [1995]). In addition, Larry Flynt, the publisher of *Hustler,* also publishes and/or distributes many other pornographic magazines, such as *Chic, Chic Letters, Family Heat, Fetish Letters, Friction, Inches, Jugs, Latin Men, Latin Women, Leg Show, Lips (New York), Male Insider, Nasty Letters, Nasty Photos, Off-Beat Letters, Oralrama!, Oriental Dolls, Over 40, Over 50, Playguy, Private Moments, Tail Ends, Torso, Uncut,* and *Wanted* (*Ulrich's,* 1995).

## Changes in Subscription Rates Over Time

Because subscription rates for 1991 were reported in the first edition of *Against Pornography,* I was astonished to find that only 4 years later this rate for *Penthouse* had dropped from 4,600,000 (National Research Bureau, 1991) in 1991 to 1,304,709 in 1995 (estimated by the senior editor of *Working Press*).[14] Since these figures are provided by the magazines, I presumed that *Penthouse* would be able to explain this enormous disparity. However, *Penthouse* spokes-

**TABLE 1.2** Subscription Rates for Selected U.S. Pornography Magazines from 1978-1997

| *Year* | *Playboy* | *Penthouse* | *Hustler* | *Oui* | *Gallery* | *Club* | *Chic* |
|---|---|---|---|---|---|---|---|
| 1978 | 6,600,000 | 4,000,000 | 2,605,000 | 1,300,000 | 800,000 | Not avail. | 450,000 |
| 1984 | 5,013,941 | 4,612,958 | 1,500,000 | 754,000 | 602,833 | 534,739 | 250,000 |
| 1988 | 3,600,000 | 4,612,958 | 1,200,000 | 395,000 | 500,000 | 600,000 | 250,000 |
| 1992 | 3,600,000 | 4,612,958 | 1,200,000 | 395,000 | 500,000 | 700,000 | 90,000 |
| 1996 | 3,400,000 | 1,304,709 | 1,200,000 | 395,000 | 500,000 | 700,000 | 50,000 |
| 1997 | 3,400,000 | Not avail. | 500,000 | 395,000 | 500,000 | 700,000 | 100,000 |
| Percentage change | –94.1 | –206.6 | –421.0 | –229.1 | –60.0 | +30.9 | –350.0 |

SOURCE: *Working Press of the Nation* (National Research Bureau, 1978-1997)

person James Martise failed to respond to telephone and fax requests to unravel this mystery.[15]

Perhaps the relatively low subscription rates for *Penthouse* in 1996 are due to the exclusion from the circulation count of other *Penthouse* publications that year: 400,000 for *Penthouse Forum;* 550,000 for *Penthouse Letters;* and 350,000 for *Forum* (National Research Bureau, 1995). In addition, a circulation figure of 3,172,898 is recorded for *Girls of Penthouse* (*Ulrich's,* 1995).

Richard Teitelbaum (1996) notes that

> *Penthouse*'s woes are similar to those bedeviling such staid publishers as *Times Mirror* and *Knight-Ridder*. Competing electronic media—in *Penthouse*'s case, vavavoom videos and XXX Internet Websites—have readers browsing elsewhere. . . .
>
> Skinzines also have distribution problems, stemming from the lingering effects of a 1990 boycott by religious groups against stores that displayed adult publications. (p. 20)

Table 1.2 presents the changes in the subscription rates for the seven best-known porn magazines for selected years between 1978 and 1997. With the exception of *Club,* this table shows that all these magazines have declined quite drastically. *Hustler* registered the greatest decline, from a high circulation of 2,605,000 in 1978 to a low of 500,000 in 1997. This represents a decline of 421%. Presumably, these declines are due to the growth in the video porn market

**TABLE 1.3** Circulation Rates for Non-U.S. Editions of *Playboy* Magazine, 1996

| *Country* | *Circulation* |
|---|---|
| Japan | 450,000 |
| Brazil | 251,000 |
| Germany | 250,000 |
| The Netherlands | 135,000 |
| Mexico | 100,000 |
| Italy | 75,000 |
| Poland | 75,000 |
| Argentina | 70,000 |
| Spain | 70,000 |
| Czech Republic | 45,000 |
| Greece | 45,000 |
| Hungary | 40,000 |
| Turkey | 35,000 |
| Taiwan | 32,000 |
| South Africa | No information |
| **TOTAL** | 1,673,000 |

SOURCE: *1996 Working Press of the Nation* (National Research Bureau, 1995).

as well as to the escalating availability of pornography on the Internet (as Teitelbaum, 1996, noted above; also see Rimm, 1995).

*Playboy, Penthouse,* and *Hustler* magazines, like many others, also publish numerous copies in other countries. The total circulation of *Playboy*'s international editions, for example, adds up to 1,673,000 (see Table 1.3).

These very substantial non-U.S. circulation rates reveal the extent to which U.S. pornography magazines are exported to the rest of the world to the detriment of women and girls in these countries. I will describe the impact of this form of cultural imperialism on females in South Africa. In 1993, I was conducting research on sexual violence in South Africa when the country opened its doors to special watered-down editions of *Playboy, Penthouse,* and *Hustler* magazines (Russell, 1994b). Three years later, the contents of these pornographic publications are no longer softened for the new South Africa. In a country which had previously been relatively pornography-free and where Western pornography is totally alien to most of its black citizens,[16] moreover a country that is frequently cited as having the highest rape rate in the world,[16] I shudder to think of the consequences of this ignorant and short-sighted policy decision by the otherwise progressive new government that came to power under Nelson Mandela in 1994 (for a critique of the government's tolerant attitude toward pornography, see Russell, in press).

### *Estimating the Percentage of American Male Consumers of Pornography Magazines*

Because many of the magazines that are sold are read by several readers, some publishers calculate the pass-along rates (the estimated number of readers per copy) for their magazines. For example, *People* magazine estimates a pass along rate of 11 while *Time* and *Newsweek* calculate rates of from 5 to 6½ per magazine (Bianchi, 1996).

Despite intense efforts, I was unable to obtain pass-along rates for pornography magazines. I surmise that these are higher than for *Time* and *Newsweek* because many men are too embarrassed to subscribe to porn magazines. For example, many do not want their girlfriends, wives, and children to know about their interest in this material, so they cannot risk its being delivered to their homes. I suspect that others are too embarrassed to purchase them in stores. In addition, boys under 18, who are forbidden by law to purchase porn magazines, are likely to contribute greatly to the pass-along rates. (The high percentage of underage boys who have been exposed to these magazines as well as other pornographic materials is documented in Part 3.) Furthermore, boys rarely have the money to subscribe to these high-priced magazines, even if their parents would tolerate them doing so.

Because there are probably many men who "read"[18] more than one of the seven porn magazines discussed in this section, we cannot simply multiply the circulation rates for each magazine by the estimated pass-along rate, then add them together, to arrive at a sound estimate of the approximate number of men in the United States who read one of them. If we assume a pass-along rate of eight for porn magazines, and that three of these estimated eight consumers per magazine read more than one of the other porn magazines, then we can simply multiply the total circulation for all seven magazines (11,048,052) by 5 to arrive at the best estimate of the approximate number of U.S. consumers who "read" at least one of these porn magazines in 1996—that is, 55,240,260 or just over 55 million.

Since men are the main consumers of these porn magazines, calculating the approximate percentage of U.S. males who have consumed one or more of the seven leading porn magazines requires knowing the number of males in the population. According to the U.S. Bureau of the Census (1996), there were 128,314,000 males in the United States in 1995 (the most recent figure available). Hence, *an estimated 43% of American males (including babies!) were exposed to at least one of the seven porn magazines in 1995.*[19]

If 43% seems an unbelievably high estimate, it may seem less so on learning that 37% of Americans—including females—reported to Gallup Poll interviewers in 1985 that they "sometimes buy or read magazines like *Playboy*" (Press et al., 1985, p. 60).

In fact, the 43% figure is likely to be a considerable underestimate, since there are hundreds more magazines than the seven that have been the focus of this analysis. Because there has been a substantial decline in the circulation rates for porn magazines over the past few years, presumably 43% represents a significant drop in the percentage of U.S. males who were exposed to one or more of these magazines a few years ago.

If a similar analysis were to be done on the percentage of males in the population who watch pornographic videos, look at pornographic material on the Internet, play pornographic computer games, engage in telephone pornography, or create their own pornography, it seems likely that the vast majority of American men are consumers of pornography in one form or another. The horrendous implications of this probability will become clearer after reading Part 2, which describes more than 100 pornographic pictures, and Part 3, which demonstrates the relationship between males' exposure to pornography and rape.

## NOTES

1. I have incorporated several of Robert Brannon's suggestions into my definition of pornography, as well as the definitions of the concepts within it. Personal communication, March 11, 1992.

2. Claude Nuridsany and Marie Pérennou are the filmmakers of *Microcosmos,* 1996.

3. These differences were significant at $p < 0.05$ (Senn & Radtke, 1986, p. 16).

4. I have used the phrase "*it appears to*" instead of "*it is intended to*" in order to avoid the difficult, if not impossible, task of establishing the intentions of the porn producers.

5. For example, members of the now-defunct organization WAVPM (Women Against Violence in Pornography and Media)—the first feminist anti-pornography organization in the United States—used to refer to record covers, jokes, ads, and

billboards as pornography when they were sexually degrading to women, even when nudity or displays of women's genitals were not portrayed (Lederer, 1980).

6. To bring attention to this attribute of pornography, WAVPM designed a sticker to deface pornography that read: "Pornography Tells Lies About Women."

7. These distortions often have serious consequences. For example, some viewers act on the assumption that the depictions are accurate and presume that there is something wrong with females who do not behave like those portrayed in pornography. This can result in verbal abuse and/or sexual assault, including rape, by males who consider that they are entitled to the sex acts that they desire or that they believe other men enjoy.

8. This is an FBI euphemism for the frequent police practice of discounting rape cases reported to them.

9. That a sizable proportion of the killing is womanslaughter is essentially obliterated by this term.

10. Malamuth and Spinner did not report the percentages of pictorials and cartoons that were found to contain sexual violence at the beginning of the 5-year period they studied. Extrapolating from their data, I calculate the 1973 figures to be approximately 1.5% for pictorials and 6.5% for cartoons (Russell, 1980, p. 233).

11. Dietz, P. E. & Sears, H. (1987/1988). Pornography and obscenity sold in "adult bookstores": A survey of 5,132 books, magazines, and films in four American cities. *Journal of Law Reform, 21* (1 & 2), 7-46. Used with permission of the author.

12. Dietz and Sears (1987/1988) consider "fisting"—colloquially referred to as "fist fucking"—to be violent because it "entails such pronounced dilation of the anus" (p. 26) as well as tissue trauma.

13. This term applies to an individual with a penis and breasts.

14. Dawn Lombardy, senior editor at *Working Press of the Nation,* reported that the circulation rate for *Penthouse* magazine was not provided by the publisher for 1996. Nevertheless, she reported the circulation rate to be 1,304,709 (Personal communication to Roberta Harmes, October 18, 1996). *Ulrich's International Periodical Directory* (1995) reported the identical figure for *Penthouse,* so this is the figure that appears in Table 1.1 and in Appendix 1, Table A.1.1.

15. The circulation department was also contacted on October 6, 1996, but failed to provide a source for the information they reported.

16. See Russell (1991) for an African woman's analysis of the impact of pornography on the rates of rape and incestuous abuse in Soweto, South Africa.

17. According to a recent United Nations report, South Africa "has the highest incidence of reported rape in the world, 10 rapes per 1,000 population per year" (Olojede, 1997, p. A13). It may also have one of the lowest rape report rates in the world. The South African police "estimate that only 2.8 per cent of all cases of rape are actually reported" (Coomaraswamy, 1997, p. 3). Since the South African police are hardly a bastion of knowledge about rape in a country that has virtually ignored the problem until recently, it is virtually certain that the report rate is considerably lower than 2.8%.

18. The word *read* is in quotes because many men are only interested in masturbating to the pictures, not reading the text—such as it is.

19. 55,240,260 times 100 divided by 128,314,000 equals 43%.

# PART II

# PORNOGRAPHIC PICTURES AS WOMAN HATRED

# PICTURING WOMAN HATRED

> The pornographers have convinced many that *their* freedom is everyone's freedom.
>
> *Dworkin and MacKinnon, 1988* (emphasis added)

Women's ignorance about the true nature of pornography is not surprising. Pornography is, after all, part of male culture, like locker rooms, fraternities, football, and powerful government bodies. When women had the opportunity to see how the Senate Judiciary Committee conducted its investigation of Anita Hill's allegations of sexual harassment by Clarence Thomas, they were outraged. The assumption that men in politics make reasonable decisions and conduct themselves in a reasonable way was shattered. Instead, women saw how unable the male senators were to transcend their self-serving biases and deal fairly with one of their own when his credibility was challenged by a woman.

For the same reasons, I want to give women the opportunity to learn about what men are looking at in their pornography magazines. Descriptions of a wide range of examples will reveal the kinds of portrayals of women and sex that turn males on in this and other male-dominated societies. Because so many men enjoy looking at pornography, seeing the material tends to lower their consciousness of its woman-hating character rather than raise it. I believe the combination of descriptions and comments on pornographic pictures presented in this book will also provide men with a more critical perspective.

I will start by presenting 23 cartoons from pornographic publications. Cartoons can be very revealing indicators of the attitudes of the publishers or managers of pornography magazines toward women and sexual assault. The vast majority of the other 100 pictures to be described and analyzed consist of photographs of real women.

Many people fool themselves into believing that the women they see in the pages of pornography are all willing or even happy to be doing this kind of work; that the rapes, beatings, and other forms of torture portrayed are only simulated; that the women in bondage are never hurt or humiliated while posing for the camera and never sexually assaulted before being released from their bonds. They may also believe that, because the women photographed have chosen to do work that is stigmatized, they are responsible for whatever befalls them.

Even were these views accurate or reasonable, which they are not, this is no reason to discount the harm caused to the *consumers* who absorb the misogynist messages conveyed by pornographic materials. In addition, it would not justify the harm that results from consumers acting out the messages they internalize from pornography. One of the reasons I chose to include cartoons was to challenge these kinds of rationalizations. Because cartoons do not involve live women, the issues of choice and harm to the women who are used in pornography cannot distract readers from recognizing the woman-hating messages in the cartoons.

On the other hand, some people might find it easier to ignore the misogyny and violence in the cartoons than in the photographs. Those who don't belong to the groups that are targeted by cartoons often say, "But they're only jokes! Where's your sense of humor?" as if humor wipes out the harmful effects of sexism and racism. This kind of rationalization is easier to refute when pornography demeans real women. In short, some readers will be more disturbed by the descriptions of cartoons while others will be more upset by the degrading portrayals of real women. Readers who manage to discount the misogyny evident in both of these kinds of pornography may have a tougher time discrediting the data and theoretical arguments presented in Part 3.

Most people probably do not consider pictures on record covers to be pornographic, but the two examples I have included in my descriptions of pornographic pictures meet my definition of pornography. Images and stories that are commonly regarded as mainstream may nevertheless qualify as pornography. Many people today mistakenly believe that *Playboy* and *Penthouse* are not pornographic magazines because looking at them has become so widely accepted. The fact that millions of males use the pictures as ejaculatory material tends to be forgotten—at least by women.[1] This is why I have included several examples from these two magazines.

Written materials are a significant part of the pornography market. Racks of inexpensive paperback novels on a wide range of pornographic themes are a staple product in many pornography stores. The covers of some of these books, as well as a few excerpts from their pages, are included in the content analysis to follow.

I have also included many examples of pornography that portray contempt, hostility, or both, toward women without depicting violence. My theory about the causal relationship between pornography and rape developed in Part 3 will show how such sentiments contribute to the undermining of some males' inhibitions against acting out their desire to rape women.

Readers may notice that many of the examples of pornography analyzed were published in the 1970s. Given that the primary goal of this book is to show the causal relationship between pornography and harm, the publication date of the material is not important. Some readers may question my inclusion of descriptions of five pictures from Denmark and two from Japan. Once again, *where* pornography is published is irrelevant to whether or not it is causally related to rape and/or other forms of violence against women and/or harm in general. It should also be remembered that there is an international trade in pornography, as a result of which foreign materials are readily available in the United States, and vice versa.

Some critics of *Against Pornography* (Russell, 1994a) accused me of including more negative images than they believe are typical of pornography. I don't believe this criticism is valid. It is analogous to a neo-Nazi arguing that the horror and devastation of anti-Semitism in Nazi Germany cannot be judged from photographs of the concentration camps because a lot of Jews weren't incarcerated in them. Some pornography celebrates extreme torture, mutilation, and sexualized femicide.[2] For those who claim that all pornography is harmless, selecting particularly violent examples would be irrelevant. It only becomes pertinent for those who acknowledge that at least some pornography *is* harmful. Once this is conceded, a laissez faire attitude to pornography becomes irresponsible.

Let us suppose, for the sake of argument, that only 5% of pornography is significantly harmful to women. Given the huge volume of pornography and its proliferation throughout society, 5% would constitute a great deal of harm. To dismiss this harm would be dangerous and irresponsible, not to mention sexist.

There may be some otherwise skeptical readers who are willing to concede that some of the more extreme examples of pornography described at the end of the content analysis section may be harmful to women. If this small concession were to be made by many of the people who currently deny that pornography has any ill effects, it would shift the public debate to a consideration of which materials are harmful and which (if any) are not, and how the answer to this question can best be determined. Such a shift would represent very significant progress.

Some readers may be disturbed to find themselves sexually aroused by viewing pornography or by reading descriptions of pornographic pictures, despite their awareness, perhaps even abhorrence, of the misogyny revealed in them. This may engender feelings of self-criticism, or even self-hatred. There are many ways in which men and women have learned to sexualize male domination and female subordination in Western societies, including becoming aroused by both subtle and blatant forms of female degradation. Given the patriarchal structure of the society in which we live, we should not be surprised that most males, and even some females, feel sexually excited by pornographic materials that celebrate sexism and woman abuse.[3]

Since this response signifies that our culture has made destructive inroads into the psyches of these individuals, as is the case for those who discover racist attitudes in themselves, it indicates the importance of fighting against pornography and racism for both personal and political reasons. There *is* reason for great concern when those who feel aroused by pornography (or racism) embrace it and become advocates or defenders of it. Many unhealthy practices are promoted in all societies, such as consumption of unnutritional foods, cigarette smoking, alcohol consumption, and spending beyond one's means. That such practices are—like pornography—encouraged in Western cultures, particularly by the advertising industry, is no reason to accept them as harmless or to have a tolerant attitude toward them. Rather, the more destructive they are found to be, the more strenuously they should be resisted, on both personal and public levels. This book provides evidence to show that pornography qualifies as deserving the most strenuous opposition we can muster.

## WHAT'S IN THE PICTURE AND WHAT DOES IT MEAN?

### *Cartoons*

**Picture 1.** A line-drawn cartoon shows two men approaching the door of an obedience school with their "pets" on leashes. One man has a small dog with a wagging tail; the other hip-looking man has a smiling woman who is "walking" on her hands and knees, doggy-style, and wagging her bottom. She is naked but for a thick S&M collar, high boots, and a cupless halter top. Source: *Chic,* September 1977.

**Comment 1.** It is easy to discount the degradation and humiliation of the woman in this cartoon because of the humor. But consider what it means to equate women with dogs in an anthropomorphic culture in which the word *bitch* is a commonly used derogatory term for a woman. Note that the woman in this cartoon is portrayed as happy being treated as a domestic animal and going to an obedience school to receive lessons in how better to obey her master.

Such flagrantly demeaning treatment of women is usually done in private or in gatherings of sadomasochists. Nevertheless, I have seen a TV documentary on sadomasochism in which a woman was treated just like the "bitch" in this cartoon except that her master was taking her on a leash to a supermarket in Ukiah, California (*S&M: One Foot Out of the Closet,* 1980). Similar scenes were shown more recently in Michelle Handelman's documentary film titled *Bloodsisters,* about the lesbian s/m leather community in San Francisco (Russell, 1996b). I also witnessed such a scene while sitting in a San Francisco coffee house in 1996.

---

**Picture 2.** A plump, large-breasted nude woman is shown standing next to a poster depicting two crudely drawn body parts: a naked behind and an elbow. An arrow labeled "A" points toward the behind and an arrow labeled "B" points toward the elbow, followed by the questions: "Which arrow points to your ass?" and "Which arrow points to your elbow?" The woman is portrayed as pondering the answers as if befuddled by these simple questions. Source: *Penthouse,* September 1984.

**Comment 2.** This cartoon reinforces the stereotype that women are so stupid that they "can't tell their ass from their elbow." The woman's nudity here is totally gratuitous.

---

**Picture 3.** Three African American men enter the front door of a house. A rotund, large-breasted African American woman stands in front of them looking demure and bewildered, her hands behind her back. One man is clutching a gun and a television set. Another man holds up a can of beer angrily and scornfully exclaiming:

> "I come home after a hard night of robbery, rape, and murder, and she gives me a light beer! Have you ever tasted light beer?!" Source: *Hustler,* March 1981.

**Comment 3**. Here, *Hustler* magazine reinforces the dangerous, racist stereotype that African American men are violent criminals and rapists.

---

**Picture 4.** A fat, ugly woman, naked from the waist down, with unshaven legs spread widely apart, is sitting on a kitchen floor while a beer-drinking man behind her pulls up her dress. Hundreds of cockroaches are swarming from all over the kitchen toward her vagina, which the artist has carefully detailed with labia and pubic hair. A TV in the background is advertising "Roach Motel" cockroach killer. The woman appears repulsed while the man, with a wicked, gleeful expression on his face, says:

> "See that [her open genitals]? It's free, and it works just as good as those expensive roach traps." Source: *Hustler,* June 1985.

**Comment 4.** This cartoon reinforces the myth that women's genitals are disgusting and smelly, particularly those of women who do not fit pornographers' narrow notions of attractive female sex objects. Pornographers tend to dichotomize women into young, attractive sex objects and ugly, fat, or old women who are portrayed as pathetic, disgusting, and contemptible sex objects.

---

**Picture 5.** An elderly man in a business suit is seated at his desk addressing his attractive young secretary, whose dress accentuates her breasts. She has a blank, professional expression on her face as her boss tells her:

> "I've just been through a brutal board meeting, Ms. Kentworth. At times like this I need solace, compassion, understanding, and the usual blow job." Source unknown.

**Comment 5.** Jokes about sexual harassment in the workplace are very common in pornography magazines. Sometimes the women are shown as willing, sometimes as distressed, and sometimes, as in this cartoon, as totally neutral. These jokes both reflect and reinforce most men's inability to understand why sexual harassment in the workplace is a very serious problem.

**Picture 6.** The bottom half of a naked woman is shown lying on a gynecologist's table, her legs raised and her feet in stirrups for a gynecological examination. At the foot of the table, an ugly, leering gynecologist is about to insert a live electrical plug into her vagina as he smirks:

> "And now, Miss Simmons, let's check the old reflexes." Source: *Penthouse,* August 1980.

**Comment 6.** The cartoonist's choice of an electrical plug implies that the gynecologist plans to turn the woman on, prompting readers' fantasies about what he might do when she becomes sexually aroused. This cartoon makes a joke out of rape by a foreign object and trivializes the sexual abuse of women by gynecologists.

◆

**Picture 7.** In this cartoon, a female secretary is bending forward over a desk with her rear in the air. Her boss has pulled up her dress, exposing her behind and legs. His pants are halfway down his legs as he stands behind her, his eyes are closed, his head is cocked upwards and away from her as he casually thrusts his penis into her. He simultaneously dictates the following words while she takes notes as if oblivious to the sexual activity:

> "Gentlemen. We here at Creative Efficiency Associates believe in the optimum use of structured time and personnel." Source: *Playboy,* January 1987.

**Comment 7.** The secretary is shown here as totally unaffected by having to service her boss's sexual desires, as if this is as much a part of her job as taking dictation from her boss. Her apparent casualness about being sexually used by her boss reinforces the widespread myth, particularly among men, that sexual harassment is harmless.

◆

**Picture 8.** A dismayed secretary with a bare behind is shown bending forward over a desk as her fully clothed boss vigorously penetrates her from behind. A Christmas holly wreath hangs on the open door through which we glimpse people dancing wildly at an office party. One of the partying men is undressing as if about to retire to another office for sex with his provocatively clad partner. The secretary appears upset as she asks her boss:

> "You mean this is the year end Christmas bonus?" Source: *Playboy.*

**Comment 8**. The victim of sexual harassment in this cartoon is at least depicted as unhappy. The question she asks her boss indicates that she is distressed by the thought that he may consider his sex act a worthy substitute for the usual monetary bonus rather than that her boss is subjecting her to sexual intercourse in a semi-public, humiliating fashion. Besides making a joke out of the serious problem of sexual harassment in the workplace, this cartoon also reinforces men's ignorance about what is wrong with sexual harassment and why it is distressing, often traumatizing, to victims.

---

**Picture 9**. The boss in this office scene is having sex with his secretary as she leans back on his office desk. The name on the door reads "J. S. Hunter." The boss's pants are down to his knees, his secretary's dress is raised, and she is looking distinctly unhappy.

> "You want equality?" he asks her. "Next time we'll do it on your desk." Source: *Playboy,* February 1979.

**Comment 9**. Naming the harassing boss in this cartoon "J. S. Hunter" signifies that he is a predator and attempts to make this seem humorous. The boss is portrayed as misconstruing his secretary's desire to be treated as an equal—meaning, in this context, that she does not want to be treated as a sex object and subjected to having sex with him. In this parody of women's rights, the boss twists the notion of equality to suit his desires, failing to see the kinds of changes that men will have to make in order for women to enjoy equality in the workplace. Many males share this man's unwillingness or inability to understand women's feelings about both sexual harassment and the meaning of equality.

**Picture 10**. Once again the secretary in this cartoon—Miss *Petting*ale—is bent over a desk doggy-style while her boss enters her from the rear. Both are in a partial state of undress to depict an office "quickie." There is a vapid smile on the woman's face as her boss asks (or reminds) her:

> "Remember that Christmas bonus I promised you, Miss Pettingale?"
> Unbeknown to her, the boss is beckoning to a crowd of men watching from the doorway behind her and patiently awaiting their turn to have intercourse with her. Source: *Penthouse,* December 1984.

**Comment 10**. At its most benign, the joke here is supposed to be that a secretary will be subjected to gang rape instead of receiving money for her Christmas bonus. The secretary's consent is irrelevant, and her predicament as she is penetrated by her boss is so degraded and powerless that any desire for privacy she might have is of no concern to these men. This is an occasion for men to show their sexual prowess, not to fret about the feelings of a lowly secretary. By presenting gang rape as a Christmas gift to a woman, this cartoon can also be seen as conveying that women enjoy being raped.

---

**Picture 11**. In the background of this cartoon, a businessman is having sex with his secretary. She is shown lying on a desk with her dress pulled up and her legs in the air as her fully clothed boss penetrates her in full view of the other office occupants. A workman is painting the sexually harassing boss's name on the door of a presumably more private office. In the foreground of this office scene, the boss tells a disconsolate employee:

> "You may have been more deserving of the promotion Simpson, but we felt that Wrightson had a greater need for the office." Source: *Playboy*.

**Comment 11**. Rewarding an employee with a promotion for flaunting his sexually exploitive behavior over a more deserving colleague conveys the management's approval of such behavior. It also suggests an inability to distinguish between office sex and sexual harassment on the job. This form of male myopia is widespread in the workplace. Not surprisingly, there is no mention of the female employee being rewarded with a private office. Women in the workplace will never get the rewards they deserve for high performance in their jobs as long as men idealize male sexual prowess and compete with each other to evoke other men's envy by demonstrating their sense of superiority in this regard.

---

**Picture 12.** In this workplace cartoon, a sexually aroused and determined boss is leaping over his desk to fling himself on his alarmed secretary—pointedly named Miss *Goodbody*—in her low-cut, tight-fitting dress. The boss's chair and trash can are tipped over, the carpet is awry, and a wall picture is askew to convey his eagerness to reach his intended victim.

> "Relax, Miss Goodbody," the boss commands his secretary. "You can't stop an idea whose time has come." Source: *Playboy,* October 1973.

**Comment 12.** *Playboy* readers are supposed to find it funny that this boss intends to have sex with his secretary regardless of her feelings, and that he directs her to relax in these circumstances. This is reminiscent of the well-known insult, "If you're going to be raped, you might as well lie back and enjoy it." Another subtext of this cartoon is that the woman's "good body" (her name) and provocative attire show that she's "asking for it."

---

**Picture 13.** In this cartoon, a male burglar is about to leave a woman's ransacked apartment with looted valuables (TV, camera, etc.) under his arms. His attractive female victim, her clothes ripped away to reveal her large naked breasts and gartered thighs, is tightly bound to a chair. Smiling sweetly at the burglar, she politely asks him:

> "Before you go, would you mind tightening my ankles a little?" Source: *Playboy,* October 1977.

**Comment 13.** Here, *Playboy* magazine reinforces the myth that women are sexual masochists who enjoy pain, even when it is inflicted by a stranger who has ransacked her home and is departing with her valuable belongings.

**Picture 14.** A man with a female companion on his arm is walking by the window of a travel agency in which a prominent advertisement reads, "Try our champagne and Gang Bang flight." The delighted man says to the woman beside him:

> "Well . . . at last the airlines have come up with something fresh!" Source: *Playboy,* November 1973.

**Comment 14.** Here the horrifying experience of gang rape is minimized by the casual use of the slang term "gang bang" and the man's description of the obnoxious, sexist ad as merely "fresh." Gang rape is normalized by both the travel agency and the man, who appears to presume that his female companion will not be offended by his enthusiasm. Men's craving for sexual novelty (freshness) accounts for their wandering eyes and penises and challenges the pornography industry to keep searching for new women to degrade in new ways.

---

**Picture 15.** A small, plump, dowdily dressed old woman carrying groceries stops on a deserted street to look at a huge billboard advertisement inscribed with the following message:

> "IF YOU HAVE BEEN RAPED OR WOULD LIKE TO BE RAPED, CALL RAPE LINE 555-7675." Source: *Hustler,* February 1981, p. 38.

**Comment 15.** Here *Hustler* magazine reinforces one of the most widespread myths: that women enjoy being raped. Pornography is a significant promoter of this pernicious lie. The choice of a plump, dowdy-looking old woman as interested in the billboard ad suggests that she may be so hard up for sex that she'd settle for rape. This message is conveyed in many ageist jokes. The notion that women would rather be raped than deprived of heterosexual sex grossly belittles the horror of rape and the trauma that it causes. It also exaggerates women's desire to be penetrated by the almighty male penis, and it insults women who deviate from men's constricted and bigoted ideas of attractive female sex objects.

**Picture 16.** Two plain-looking women are jogging through a park together as one says to the other:

> "The trouble with rapists is that they're never around when you need them." Source: *Hustler,* December 1990.

**Comment 16.** Once again, *Hustler* magazine promotes the myth that women enjoy being raped. This cartoon ridicules the reality that women jog to keep fit and strong, and that many feel compelled to jog with one or more companions to lessen the risk of being raped, kidnapped, and/or murdered by a man. The punch line mocks the empowerment many women feel through physical activity and the fact that some women also engage in such activities the better to defend themselves against rapists and other predatory men.

---

**Picture 17.** A dishevelled woman is lying face-up on a deserted path with her back propped up against a broken wooden fence. It is nighttime, and the woman has just been violently raped by an evil-looking stranger. He is pulling up his pants as he runs away from the scene of his crime. The violent nature of the assault is conveyed by the woman's dishevelled appearance: her panties still circle one of her knees; her dress is bunched up around her waist, exposing her breasts and vagina; her purse is lying in the middle of the path; and the rapist's hat lies upturned on the grass. Out of the mouth of the woman comes one French word: "ENCORE" (Again). Source: *Penthouse.*

**Comment 17.** Stranger rape is much more apt to be taken seriously by the law and the public than rape by a date, a husband, or an acquaintance. In addition, the more violent the rape, the more credible and grievous it is seen to be. These facts don't stop *Penthouse* magazine from using humor to suggest that women also enjoy being violently raped by strangers.

---

**Picture 18.** A pajama-clad man is humped over a woman in bed, suggesting that he is engaged in intercourse. Her eyes are closed as the man apologizes to her,

"I'm sorry," he says, "I didn't mean to wake you." Source: *Playboy.*

**Comment 18.** The man in this cartoon apologizes for waking the woman, not for raping her. Like him, many people do not realize that intercourse with a woman who is unable to consent constitutes rape in many states in the United States. This means that a man who penetrates a woman when she is asleep is guilty of rape. Yet many men believe they are entitled to have sex with their partner, particularly a wife, even when she is sleeping. This now out-dated view was legally correct before marital rape was criminalized in most states in the 1970s and 1980s.

---

**Picture 19.** A jovial, fully dressed man is about to complete his task of tying a naked, spread-eagled woman to the four corners of a bedstead.

> "Comfy?" he asks her.
>
> It is impossible to see the woman's expression in this cartoon because her face is hidden by her unruly hairdo. Source: *Playboy,* December 1975.

**Comment 19.** Because the woman's willingness to be tied up is suggested by the man's concern for her comfort, this cartoon reinforces the prevalent yet dangerous myth that women are masochists who enjoy bondage. While some women *are* into the masochistic role in sadomasochistic sex, the majority of women repudiate this sexual practice. Most women in bondage lose whatever power they would otherwise have to prevent abuse in sexual situations, which, of course, is why some males enjoy the fantasy and/or the practice of tying women up.

---

**Picture 20.** Two men who are obviously intent on rape are starting to undress as one of them tells a provocatively dressed, but clearly alarmed, young woman:

> "Well, I'm a consenting adult and Charley here is a consenting adult—that makes two out of three." Source: *Playboy,* April 1973.

**Comment 20.** This cartoon is not about women liking to be raped; the about-to-be raped young woman has already made it clear that she is not interested in having sex with the men, and her body language confirms her rejection of their overtures. It is about men feeling entitled to rape. Males' sense of entitlement to impose their sexual desires on girls and women is very common and a significant factor in many rapes.

---

**Picture 21.** A helpless woman in a skimpy and revealing dress is tied down on railway tracks. A train has stopped in the middle of the tracks and two members of the train crew are shown running toward her. They begin to pull off their overalls as they approach the woman, suggesting that they are planning to rape her. Source: *Playboy,* September 1971.

**Comment 21.** *Playboy* readers are supposed to find it humorous that train workers have stopped a train, not to rescue but to rape a defenseless woman. In reality, many men take advantage of women and girls who are vulnerable or helpless, sometimes even posing as good Samaritans by offering to help them out of some unpleasant situation, then raping them.

---

**Picture 22.** This drawing shows a naked man standing next to a bed with an intense, crazed expression on his face. He is holding a shocked-looking naked woman over his genital area as he penetrates her vagina. Her legs are wrapped around his waist, her head and arms are thrown back, her fingers are splayed and rigid suggesting shock, as the head of the man's penis protrudes from her mouth. Source unknown.

**Comment 22.** This picture illustrates a popular male fantasy that the bigger a man's penis is, the better. This weird notion ignores the fact that intercourse with men with large penises can be painful to some women, particularly when men thrust them back and forth aggressively. If the picture showed a man penetrating a woman's entire body with a weapon, it would probably amuse fewer males. But if it's a penis that does the damage, it's considered masculine and humorous.

---

**Picture 23.** In this line drawing, a woman whose large breasts are exposed is grimacing in agony as a man standing in front of her sticks a long needle into her left breast. Thirteen other needles have been inserted into her right breast. A safety pin has been thrust through one of her nipples. Rope around her neck and arms indicate that she is in a state of bondage. Her smiling torturer, who is holding her with one arm, appears to be enjoying his piercing project. A woman who is also smiling stands behind the victim. The man and the woman are both attractive, conservatively dressed, and appear to be collaborating in the torture of this woman. Source unknown.

**Comment 23.** The inclusion of a smiling woman in this drawing, as well as her and the man's attractive well-dressed appearance, serves to normalize and legitimize the torture in which the man is engaged. The insertion of needles into women's breasts and other body parts has become an increasingly popular genre in pornography, as well as in the so-called leather community (a euphemism for sadomasochists).[4]

## *Racist and Anti-Semitic Pornography*

Racist pornography is an identifiable genre in this medium that has been ignored by most politically progressive people, including some feminists. Because of sexism and because most liberals and radicals have been brainwashed into believing that pornography is harmless, this pernicious material is trivialized as merely about sex rather than about eroticizing sexist racism. The element of sex makes it *more,* not *less,* dangerous.

**Picture 24.** In this photograph, the head of an African American woman is shown in profile with a thick, elongated, serpent-like tongue protruding from her mouth. The caption under the picture reads,

> "They say women are all vipers." Source: *Playboy.*

**Comment 24.** A viper is a snake, and when people are referred to as vipers, the epithet has treacherous or venomous connotations. Despite the fact that the caption refers to all women, the picture is of an African American woman. The depiction of an African American woman as a viper reinforces a sexist and racist myth that associates evil with blackness and womanhood. It also exemplifies the fact that African American women are frequently depicted in pornography as animalistic or as animals—with the associated connotations of being inferior, wild, savage, dangerous, devouring, or even deadly.

---

**Picture 25.** The illustration on the cover of a book titled *Animal Sex Among Black Women* (part of a pornographic book series called "Animal Journals") depicts a naked African American woman masturbating as she lies on the ground with her parted legs in the air, her rear facing the viewer. A cloth is loosely bound around her legs and a look of sexual pleasure suffuses her face. A large Labrador retriever is heading toward her. Source: *Animal Sex Among Black Women* (American Art Enterprises, North Hollywood, California), 1983.

**Comment 25.** The male author of *Animal Sex Among Black Women* alleges that African American women have a particular propensity for sex with animals.

> "When I began to exhaustively research the topic of the black female," he writes, in an attempt to establish scientific credentials where none exist, "I discovered that a lot of them, caught up in the escapist syndrome . . . had taken to having sex with animals."

This pornographer's pretense that *Animal Sex* is a serious, research-based book, despite the pornographic language on every page, reinforces the racist and sexist views of readers who may well not realize the fraudulence of the author's claim that it is based on research.

---

**Picture 26.** The cover of another pornographic book, titled *Abuse: Black & Battered,* shows a muscular, shirtless African American man standing in front of a bed with a stranglehold on a small African American teenage girl dressed in her underclothes. The man is using his free hand to pull at the girl's bra, exposing one of her breasts. This picture appears to be depicting an incestuous attack—allegedly based on "a tape-recorded interview"—described on the back cover in the following words:

> I'll never forget the night my father came into my room and forced me to do those terrible things to him! That night, when I ran away after he slapped

me, he came after me. He tied me, stripped me and raped me, telling me I'd better get to love it, telling me I'd better get used to it. Source: *Abuse: Black & Battered* (New York: Star Distributors), 1981.

**Comment 26.** *Abuse: Black & Battered* purports to be one in a series of case study-based books in "Dr. Lamb's Library." The pornographic language, the absence of a named author, the "adults only" label, and the admission inside the book that "All characters in this book are fictional . . ." confirm the fact that the stories are a sham. Nevertheless, the feigned authenticity appears to be designed for readers who get off on "true accounts." The book opens with the following racist passage:

> There is a myth about life in the ghetto, and the resulting attitudes about the sexual relationships between ghetto people. The myth says that all sex is abusive sex, but behind every myth, there is some truth.

This is a convoluted way of saying that abusive sex, like the incestuous attack depicted on the cover, is particularly prevalent among African Americans who live in ghettos. Since the manifest purpose of pornography is to arouse men sexually, this means that satisfied readers of *Abuse: Black & Battered* likely masturbate to stories of African American women being raped, beaten, and sexually abused by African American men.

The cover story about a young girl being sexually abused by her father is an example of child pornography. Although pictorial child pornography is illegal in the United States, authors of pornographic novels and short stories (as in this book) are at liberty to depict children engaged in all manner of sex acts with adults, other children, and/or animals. *Abuse: Black & Battered* is one of many books that aims to turn men on to racist and sexist depictions of sexual abuse, including criminal acts against children.

---

**Picture 27.** The cover picture of *Soul Slave,* another racist and sexist book in a series of pornographic "Punishment Books," shows a dark-skinned African American woman sitting on a trash can. Her clothes have been pulled aside to reveal her breasts, upper thighs, and genital area. Rope crisscrosses her body, tightly circling both of her breasts, her waist, ankles, and pelvic area. A clothespin is attached to one nipple, a taut rope to the other. Her lipstick-covered lips are parted, her eyes closed, suggesting enjoyment of her predicament. The following passage appears on the back cover:

> When the white man tied the ropes around me, I moaned with a deep sense of satisfaction in my heart. I felt the ropes cutting into my wrists and I shivered with desire. I was just a nigger bitch, and this white man knew just how a nigger bitch should be treated. Source: *Soul Slave* (New York: Star Distributors), 1981.

**Comment 27.** The racist misogyny reflected on the back cover of *Soul Slave,* by an author using the name Rita Cochran, is even more grotesque inside. For example:

> Rance [a white man] looked down at me and said, "Get naked, Nigger!" And those words were like the greatest poetry in the world to me. . . . It was like that man had dug down there in the deepest part of me and found something that was ultimate nigger, ultimate bitch, ultimate pain-loving whore.
>
> "I am going to give you the fucking of your worthless, nigger life," he said. . . . Then he cleared his throat and spit at me. A glob of spittle landed on one of my big, nigger tits. . . . I had never felt more alive in my life, my worthless, nigger life. . . . One of them [white boys] told me that I was a special nigger, that I could take more cock into my pussy than any dozen Southern belles. I thought about that and it gave me pride. There was little else that I could be proud of.

This racist garbage is reminiscent of the raping of slave women by plantation owners in the southern United States. The male fantasy that slave women enjoyed being raped and degraded magnifies the offensiveness of this pornographic book. It is shocking and mystifying that even people who are concerned about racism continue to ignore such material.

---

**Picture 28.** This is an aerial view of a naked white woman lying spread-eagled on her back on the floor, a chain across one leg. She is surrounded by five naked African American men, four of whom are lying on their stomachs and holding her in place. One of the men has his hand very close to her crotch. The woman's face, turned to one side, is expressionless, perhaps even unconscious. Source: *Hustler,* May 1978.

**Comment 28.** This depiction of the imminent gang rape of a white woman by African American men is used to illustrate a story titled "Belle of the Ball." In this story, a white woman sexually entices African American men while visiting their slave quarters. The woman then becomes the men's shackled slave. This story reverses the historical reality of white men invading the slave quarters on their plantations and raping their African American women and girl slaves. It also promotes the prevalent myth that African American men are sexual predators with a particular craving for white women.

---

**Picture 29.** A naked white woman is being penetrated from behind, doggy-style, by a naked African American man. Her face is not visible in this photograph because her head is being held and pressed into the pelvic area of a second African American man. Presumably, she is being forced to perform fellatio on him. The caption for this rape scene reads as follows:

> "Rape fans will get off on black revolutionaries feeding their white captive at both ends in *Hot Summer*." Source: Photo from movie *Hot Summer*.

**Comment 29.** This picture portrays one of the most common racist stereotypes in white American culture: that African American males are particularly prone to rape white women. The reference to "black revolutionaries" in the caption may be intended to suggest that these men are motivated to seek social change in the United States in order to have access to white women.

The term "rape fans" normalizes rape and treats it as a spectator sport. Notice also that the caption completely ignores the woman's feelings and the horror and harmful effects of rape, and invites male viewers to do the same. The woman is treated as a nonhuman object by the men in the picture and by the pornographer who wrote the caption.

---

**Picture 30.** The cover picture for *Sluts of the S.S.*—a book in a series called "War Horrors"—shows a woman at the feet of an S.S. officer, grasping his legs with her hands and licking his boots. Her skirt is pulled up to expose her bare buttocks, one cheek of which is adorned with a swastika tattoo. Source: *Sluts of the S.S.* (New York: Star Distributors), 1979.

**Comment 30.** Pornography with Nazi themes is an identifiable genre in Western pornography. *Sluts of the S.S.* sexualizes atrocities during the Nazi era. It contains descriptions of the repeated rape and torture of a Jewish woman by a Nazi who orders her,

> "On your knees, Jewish dog";
> "You will learn to obey the Master Race";
> "You will suck the dick of the master. . . . Open your Jewish mouth."
> And,
> "Whore," he yelled. "You will love the cock of your master."

The Jewish "heroine" ends up with a young Nazi as her lover.

Describing Jewish women Holocaust victims of forced prostitution and femicide as "sluts" is an outrageous victim-blaming misnomer. Portraying them as loving to be sexually brutalized, humiliated, and tortured by S.S. men who were their most hated enemies is consistent with one of the most popular pornographic lies: that women love to be hurt, used, and defiled by men.

Eroticizing anti-Semitism was one of the strategies deliberately used by Hitler to foster Gentile Germans' hatred toward Jews. It is very frightening to realize that there continues to be a wide market for this kind of bigoted material in the United States today.

---

**Picture 31.** The cover picture on an anti-Semitic paperback titled *Hitler's Sex Doctor* features a naked, tightly bound woman kneeling on the floor. A giant swastika hangs in the background. Behind the woman is a large bald man with a goatee who appears to be threatening her life as he pulls at a noose around her neck and holds a long blade to her throat. At the bottom of the cover is the following announcement:

> PERSONAL ADS. Ten pages of ads [inside the book] from people who want to meet you [the reader]. Source: *Hitler's Sex Doctor*.

**Comment 31.** The use of Hitler's name in the title of this book is entirely gratuitous; presumably it has a special appeal for anti-Semites. The personal ads in *Hitler's Sex Doctor* facilitate alliances between anti-Semitic readers. Bigots of this persuasion may well have used this pornography book and others like it to organize pro-Nazi or anti-Semitic groups. If this is the case, it would mean that stories of sexual violence against women are being used as the vehicle for organizing such groups.

---

**Picture 32.** In this picture, a uniformed Hitler look-alike with a stern expression on his face has his hand raised to spank the bare behind of a woman who is bent over his knee. The thigh-high stockings, garter belt, and stiletto heels so popular with many pornography consumers are all that the viewer can see of this woman besides her bare buttocks. A swastika is visible on one of the sleeves of the man's uniform. Source: *Oui.*

**Comment 32.** It is gruesome to think that a pornographer would use a Hitler look-alike in a picture designed to excite men sexually. Eroticizing a genocidal dictator whose macho desire to conquer the world culminated in World War II mocks the millions of victims, survivors, and sufferers of this agonizing historical period. It is also profoundly disturbing to see sexual violence against women being used to eroticize the Holocaust.

---

**Picture 33.** In a cover photo of a pornography magazine titled *Swastika Snatch,* two naked young women are sitting on a bare mattress in prison waiting to be tortured by two uniformed Nazi soldiers. A small photograph superimposed on an upper corner of the cover shows one of the prisoners shackled to a wall while a female Nazi soldier presses her bare buttocks into the prisoner's face. The text in the lower corner of this picture reads,

> "They became willing sex slaves to the strange fantasies of their captors."
> Source: *Swastika Snatch,* Vol. 1, No. 1.

**Comment 33.** Female sexual slavery is a common theme in pornography. The female victims are often portrayed as willing, even eager, to be enslaved. This cover picture provides an example of this grotesque male fantasy. If African American people were depicted in contemporary non-pornographic publications as willing or eager to be enslaved by white people, politically progressive people would likely engage in vociferous protest.

Many men get sexually excited by seeing pictures of women having sex together. Some become sexually aroused when sex between women is abusive, as in this picture. It is not correct, however, to consider portrayals of woman-on-woman sex in pornography as lesbian sex, because the men who make heterosexual pornography do not understand lesbian sex, and heterosexual women are often required or forced to perform these scenes.

Quite often, woman-on-woman sex is used in pornography as a prelude to the "real" thing—heterosexual sex. The women are already turned on when the man takes over to show them what superior sex with a male is all about. The "lesbians" are typically required to appear sexually aroused and satisfied by him. Some analysts maintain that this setup frees the male viewer from vicarious performance anxiety because the man in these scenarios is not responsible for sexually arousing the females.

---

**Picture 34.** A 4-feet, 10-inch naked plastic blow-up doll with "3 functional love openings" is displayed in an ad published in *Hustler*. The doll's legs are spread apart, revealing a hairless genital area. Large letters across the top of the ad read:

> "From the Land of Diminutive People Comes Kim, Your Own Personal LITTLE CHINA DOLL."

Then, in smaller letters:

> I'm small . . . but I know all I need to know to make you very happy in bed. In Hong Kong, where I come from, a girl learns very early how to please a man.
>
> I've got a 7-inch deep vagina with little tingly spots that drive a man wild. Out back I have a six inch rear channel that is so snug and tight it will squeeze the juice out of you on those nights when you want something different. And, of course, I just love to suck and take deep throat. . . .
>
> And to make our encounters even more interesting . . . you can get me with the special Virgin Vagina option. It gives me a "cherry" you can pop and a super tight fit that makes every time my first time. Source: *Hustler,* Vol. 7, No. 9, 1981.

All this for a cost of only $19.95!

**Comment 34.** So-called "fuck dolls" are frequently advertised in pornographic magazines. Available by mail order or in pornography stores, "Little China Doll" reveals common racist stereotypes about Asian women as extremely submissive and trained to serve and "please a man." As well as being detrimental to Asian and Asian American women, the use of this stereotype in this context informs women in general that men are primarily interested in docile, virginal women who love nothing better than to serve men. This is certainly depressing news for heterosexual women and places them in a serious dilemma. How submissive must they be to have relationships with men?

The description of "Little China Doll" makes her sound more like a girl than a woman: her small size, her name, her hairless genital area. This ad may well be appealing to pedophiles and men who find adolescent girls sexually alluring.

The fact that there are business establishments advocating that men use plastic blow-up dolls as a substitute for women, and that there are male consumers who buy these products, conveys the message that it is women's sexuality above all else that men value. The marketability of these dolls also provides a dramatic demonstration of men's capacity to separate their sexual desires from love, respect, and affection; indeed, it trades on men's ability to objectify women. It also shows how unimportant sexual reciprocity is for some men. Plastic dolls are the literal sex objects that many women have reproved men for treating them as.

---

**Picture 35.** This photograph shows a frontal view of a naked Asian woman from her thighs to her head. She is standing with her arms tightly bound behind her back and her head drooping lifelessly toward one of her shoulders. She is also bound around her waist. A double strand of rope attached to the rope at her waist descends to her vulva and cuts deeply between her labia. A sinister-looking Asian man is holding a flaming coal with which he appears to be about to burn the helpless woman. Source: *Cherry Blossom,* No. 3 (Los Angeles: Utopia Publishing Company), March 1977.

**Comment 35.** Asian women are a favorite target of bondage and torture in pornographic magazines. The words "Cherry Blossoms" are often used in pornography to represent Asian women, perhaps because of the association of cherry blossoms with Japan or the fact that the word *cherry* symbolizes innocence and virginity and that flowers are associated with women.

What percentage of men, one wonders, are turned on by the idea of a woman being deliberately burned? Is pornography involving Asian women intended mostly for Asian men, or for men of other ethnic identities? Do sadistic pornographic depictions as exemplified in this picture have particular appeal for American soldiers whose anti-Asian racism was fostered during the Vietnam War? Research needs to address these questions.

◆

**Picture 36.** A close-up of an Asian woman's face has been photographed 2 inches or so away from an erect penis. She is holding the penis and appears to have been engaged in fellatio. She looks revolted as semen drips from her mouth. Source: *Oriental Pussy.*

**Comment 36.** It is rare that pornographers publish pictures portraying such obvious expressions of female revulsion toward one of men's favorite sex acts. Most males prefer to believe that women become sexually excited by the sight of this part of their anatomy, and that they enjoy whatever sex acts males care to inflict on them, including having sperm excreted over their faces or into their mouths.

Could it be that some men would find this woman's revulsion exciting because it constitutes evidence of the man's domination of her? After all, if she enjoys doing fellatio on him, maybe he isn't really in command. And why should he care if she doesn't enjoy it, anyhow? Revolting her could satisfy the sadist in him, just as many men prefer rape over consensual intercourse.

◆

**Picture 37.** A frightened-looking Asian woman with dark circles around her eyes and a thick gag over her mouth is featured in this photograph. Rope is bound around her neck and the upper half of her body (her lower half is not shown), and her arms are tied behind her back. Source unknown.

**Comment 37.** This picture is one of a series that focuses on the bondage of this Asian woman. The text that accompanies this picture reads:

> He had made no bones about the fact that he had a fetish for Orientals. She found that disgusting, but she was interested in his obvious excitement. It was the first time since she arrived in this strange land that any man had paid attention.

By the end of this series, the woman is portrayed as a totally accommodating victim:

> It was ugly and sordid, but . . . it was his pleasure to do this, and if she could accept that, she could share his pleasure. She vowed to have fun.

Many men want women to be their compliant sexual slaves in real life. The common stereotype of Asian women in the United States is that they are docile, submissive, obedient, quiet, uncomplaining, and passive, as well as sweet and innocent. This makes them appear to be the perfect candidates for sexual enslavement by men who cannot tolerate the more liberated white and African American women in the United States today. This is why Asian women (including Filipinas) are particularly popular with men who participate in mail-order bride programs. These men fail to comprehend that many of these young women have been forced to appear accommodating because of their impoverished economic circumstances.

---

**Picture 38.** This photo shows another Asian woman in very heavy bondage as she straddles a ladder in which both her legs are tied apart. She has a ball gag in her mouth and her arms are tightly swaddled together. Although her breasts are visible and unbound, her genitals are inaccessible because of her position astride the ladder and the tightness of her bonds. Source unknown.

**Comment 38.** There is considerable bondage and torture pornography that caters to males who become aroused by pictures portraying the domination, humiliation, and/or brutalization of women without showing any genital sexual acts. Some s/m advocates argue that obtaining sexual gratification from sadomasochistic encounters that don't involve genital or anal penetration is a form of safe sex. The same, presumably, applies to male sadists who act out on women who are not into s/m. These practices may prevent catching AIDS, but they do not prevent physical or psychological injury to the victims.

**Picture 39.** This cover picture of *Latin Babes,* a pornographic magazine that features Latin women, shows a young woman seated in a chair with her legs spread open, giving the consumer a frontal view of her crotch. Although she is wearing an exotic beaded Middle-Eastern-looking headdress, she is also munching candy, which gives her the appearance of an adolescent girl. The word *babes* in the magazine's title also contributes to her infantilization. Aside from the title, there is nothing about the young woman that identifies her as Latin. Source: *Latin Babes,* Vol. II, No. 1.

**Comment 39.** The text inside *Latin Babes* reads as follows:

> Hot Salsa or Sweet Salsa, however you like your Latino [should be Latina] babes, we've got 'em. These cuties are so sweet to look at, so soft to touch, but so-so hot to fuck.

Salsa is a spicy Mexican sauce eaten with Mexican food. Using the word *salsa* to describe Latina women objectifies them as mere sauce. Describing them as "so-so hot to fuck" plays off the stereotype that Latinas are eager and passionate about sex with men—despite their sweet and innocent appearance.

**Picture 40.** An attractive Latina with enormous bare breasts (a tribute to silicon, no doubt) is supposed to be working out in a gym. She was the "Playmate of the Month" centerfold for *Playboy* magazine in November 1984. Her tiny, tightly stretched workout garment fails to cover her pubic hair or her breasts. Her hands are placed on the cross bar of an arm-strengthening exercise machine attached to a chain suspended from above. A pole connecting the base of the apparatus to the upper part of the machine is positioned to look as if it is entering her vagina and skewering her. The apparatus with its chain and poles are reminiscent of sadomasochistic paraphernalia. Source: *Playboy,* November 1984.

**Comment 40.** Aside from her name, there is nothing that identifies this *Playboy* centerfold as Latina. *Playboy* and *Penthouse* have been criticized along with the beauty pageant industry for consistently choosing white women to grace their pages. They responded to this criticism by including a few token men and women of color on their pages from time to time. However, they have tended to select very light-skinned women with Caucasian-like features. The rare Latina women whom they choose often look indistinguishable from Caucasians, as is the case with the subject of this picture. This, plus the tokenism, is symptomatic of the racist equation of whiteness with attractiveness and desirability typical of these magazines and of most pornography.

This photograph could be an exaggerated version of an ad for Nautilus exercise fitness clubs. These clubs typically use thin sexy models in revealing outfits to try to manipulate women into believing that they, too, can look like the model if only they will join the club. Women are supposed to be motivated by wanting to improve their looks for men, rather than for their own health, well-being, or enjoyment.

---

**Picture 41.** The cover of an X-rated video game titled *Custer's Revenge* depicts a cartoon caricature of a disheveled Yankee soldier with a naked behind, panting and sweating with sexual desire. The soldier is superimposed on a picture in which a beautiful and shapely Native American woman, her cleavage and thighs exposed, is loosely tied to a totem pole. A tepee in the background augments the Native American motif. Notification that the video is "not for sale to minors" appears at the bottom of the picture. Source: Video game *Custer's Revenge* (produced by American Multiple Industries).

**Comment 41.** *Custer's Revenge* is a video game in which male figures with erections move through a maze and score points by raping a Native American woman. The player who accomplishes the most rapes wins. The sexism and racism inherent in this game is so extreme that it ignited considerable protest. The horrendous betrayal and near extermination of Native Americans by the early white settlers in the United States accentuates the gross insensitivity of *Custer's Revenge.* The fact that many Native American women were raped as well as murdered at this time further exacerbates the offensiveness of this video game. Because of the vociferous protests mounted against *Custer's Revenge,* happily it enjoyed a very short shelf life.

## *Photographic Pornography*

While the section on racist pornography included several photographs of women of color, many of the pictures were drawings. With few exceptions, the pictures to follow are photographs of women. This distinction is extremely important because pornographic photographs of women and children are records of their abuse and degradation. This point has to be emphasized to counter the oft-repeated claim that pornographic pictures are merely "images" and that pornography in general is mere fantasy. This fiction is used to bolster the erroneous contention that pornography is harmless.

**Picture 42.** This photograph is one of a series titled "Uses for Women." In it a naked woman lies atop a bar counter with her head unseen and her buttocks and shaved vulva sticking up in the air toward the viewer. A serious-looking bartender, smartly dressed in vest and bow tie, is using her genitals to open a beer bottle. A caption below the picture reads, "A Handy Bottle Opener." The two men in this photograph are depicted as completely unfazed by the use of the woman's vagina to open bottles and the graphic view of her genitals a couple of feet away from their faces. The text accompanying the picture reads,

> Since time began women have complained, "You're just using me for sex!" Don't get the impression that HUSTLER magazine thinks of women only as sex objects. Women can be used for many other things. Source: *Hustler*.

**Comment 42.** The kind of contempt for women displayed in this picture is one of the hallmarks of *Hustler* magazine. Mocking feminist criticism and goals is another. In this cartoon, for example, Larry Flynt acknowledges feminists' objections to men treating women as sex objects. However, he doesn't argue that this is harmless or that *Hustler* magazine is not guilty of doing this. He says, in effect,

> Yes. At *Hustler* magazine we *do* treat women as sex objects. But we also treat them as substitutes for material objects, like bottle openers and other useful things.

Instead of trying to placate women, Flynt thereby ups the ante by insulting and ridiculing women even more.

**Picture 43.** This photograph is a close-up of a pretty woman's face with her mouth replaced by a replica of a gigantic vulva surrounded by masses of pubic hair. The text below the picture, titled "Lip Service," reads as follows:

> There are those who say that illogic is the native tongue of anything with tits. . . . It comes natural to many broads; just like rolling in shit is natural for dogs. . . . They speak not from the heart but from the gash, and chances are that at least once a month your chick will stop you dead in your tracks with a masterpiece of cunt rhetoric. . . . The one surefire way to stop those feminine lips from driving you crazy is to put something between them—like your cock, for instance. Source: *Hustler.*

**Comment 43.** This is another example of *Hustler* magazine's blatant and vulgar contempt for women. Many women in intimate relationships with men complain that men don't listen to them, and many men complain that women talk too much. Not surprisingly, *Hustler* magazine represents the male point of view in advocating that men use their penises to silence women. Since women's consent is seen as irrelevant in this scenario, the advice that men should use fellatio to silence women amounts to advocating oral rape. This picture also reinforces the widespread male myth that women are irrational and driven by hormones. Meanwhile, it is men who are busy destroying the planet in the name of progress. Surely *this* is a supreme example of irrationality.

---

**Picture 44.** This photo portrays a woman whose right breast has been flattened by getting caught in an old-fashioned wash wringer. She appears to be in great pain. The text below the photo refers to the woman as a "careless cunt" who "probably had her mind on humping Robert Redford." Source: *Hustler,* October 1976.

**Comment 44.** The saying that "she's really got her tit in the wringer" means that a woman is in some kind of serious trouble. This expression provides Flynt with the opportunity to portray it graphically as a "joke." Although the woman's squashed breast and pained expression are simulated, it is difficult to comprehend what is supposed to be funny about this picture.

This applies to most of the so-called jokes in pornographic magazines. After all, they are written to appeal to misogynists, as is also the description of the woman as a "careless cunt." In this instance, readers are expected to be amused by a sadistic picture of a woman suffering excruciating pain as a result of an accident.

---

**Picture 45.** Titled "Nasal Sex," this photograph is a close-up frontal view of the top half of a naked woman. Her lips are parted suggesting a smile as she looks up at a man who is wiping his penis on a towel (his face is not included in the picture). The woman's left nostril is grotesquely distorted and expanded to about two inches in diameter, with gobs of mucous dripping from it. The text accompanying this photo reads,

> When her three holes become tiresome, pack the nasal passage. A little snot helps a big prick go a long way. Source: *Hustler,* February 1991.

**Comment 45.** Referring to a woman's vagina, anus, and mouth as "three holes," as if their primary purpose is to provide gratifying penetration experiences for men's penises, is profoundly sexist and contemptuous of women.

This picture portrays the woman as a sexual slave whose role it is to service males' sexual needs with a smile, no matter how much pain and indignity this entails for her. The fact that penetration of a nasal passage—were it possible—would be devoid of sexual pleasure for women illuminates how irrelevant women's sexual desires and needs are to pornographers whose primary goal is to sexually arouse their male customers to the point of ejaculation.

---

**Picture 46.** A man wearing a chef's hat and an apron is shown in a kitchen next to a stove and a giant pot. He is clutching the neck of a small naked woman with a pair of tongs, having just lifted her out of the pot. The woman is covered from head to toe with slimy baking mix (batter) and appears to be shocked and frightened. The title of this picture is "Battered Wives," and the text reads as follows:

> This photo shows why it's no wonder that wife-beating has become one of society's stickiest problems! But today's liberated women should have expected this kind of response when they decided that men should do more of the domestic chores like cooking. Still, there's absolutely no excuse for doing something this bad. Now he's going to have to beat her just to smooth out all those lumps. Source: *Hustler,* March 1981.

**Comment 46.** This photo, including the use of the "battered wives" pun for the title, completely trivializes woman battering. This photo-cum-text is an anti-feminist political statement advocating that women stop seeking liberation and return to domesticity. It warns women that men will respond violently to their demands for equality. Many men *have* reacted to women's growing independence and assertiveness by being violent, including men in the pornography industry. The use of humor makes the threat to women who rock the patriarchal boat seem more socially acceptable.

---

**Picture 47.** This cover photo of an issue of a porn magazine called *Hard Boss* shows an attractive young woman kneeling on an office chair and leaning over the back of it, her dress pulled up to her waist exposing her gartered thigh-high stockings and bare buttocks. A young man wearing nothing but a shirt is penetrating her from behind as he holds her hips in place. The name of the magazine conveys that the parties in this sexual encounter are a boss and his secretary, which is to say that it is a depiction of sexual harassment. The woman has an ecstatic expression on her face, indicating that she is thoroughly enjoying being exploited. Source: *Hard Boss.*

**Comment 47.** This porn magazine sexualizes the boss/secretary relationship. On the inside cover of the magazine, the secretary is described as "aching with desire" for her boss and as the initiator of their sexual encounter. Many men presumably find this inaccurate portrayal of the typical sexual harassment scenario an exciting masturbatory fantasy. This depiction of sex in the office is a male illusion that seriously distorts the widespread sexual harassment of female secretaries by their male bosses and ignores the often-devastating consequences to the victims. It also promotes the idea that women may often be responsible for initiating sexual relationships with their bosses, as if this would disqualify such encounters as cases of sexual exploitation.

---

**Picture 48.** This photo shows the midsection of a naked man whose penis is about to penetrate the vagina of an attractive woman who is lying on a couch. She is naked from the waist down with her legs spread apart exposing her vulva. Her eyes are shut, her mouth is open, and she appears to be in ecstasy. The text reads,

> "Give her your best shot—and the stupid bitch will never complain again!"
> Source: ?*Bitches Who Like it Rough,* Vol. 1, No. 1.[5]

**Comment 48.** The notion that complaining women will be both silenced and satisfied by "a good fuck" is a familiar component of male mythology. Actually, the combination of sex and contempt portrayed here is antithetical to the kind of sex and caring most women desire. Note the violent connotation in the equation of good sex with a man's "best shot." Indeed, the assurance that his best shot will stop the woman from ever complaining again can also be read as a covert message that it will kill her. The overt contempt and hostility expressed in the text (referring to the woman as a "stupid bitch") lends added credibility to this interpretation.

---

**Picture 49.** This photo shows a close-up view of a woman's vulva as she lies on her back, her stockinged legs wide open and a big smile plastered on her face. In keeping with a common pornographic convention, the woman is pulling her labia apart with her hands in order to enhance the graphic display of her crotch for the male viewer. A man's hands are aiming a huge fire hose nozzle toward her rectum. Source: *Swank,* March 1984.

**Comment 49.** This photo is the last in a series titled "Fireman's Ball." It is preceded by several scenes of intercourse and oral sex between a fireman and a woman he is rescuing. The woman is supposed to be so sexually insatiable that she eagerly awaits the insertion of a fire hose nozzle into her anus or vagina. Turning on the hose would certainly cause her great discomfort. Women who enjoy a lot of sex are often threatening to men who like to think that their sexual interest and capacity is greater than women's. Maybe the hose is the only thing that can "put out" her alleged insatiability.

This picture-cum-text reinforces the idea that women enjoy being penetrated by huge foreign objects. Perhaps it also reinforces men's erroneous belief that women—rather than men—crave gigantic penises. All the better to express aggression with.

The common sight in pornographic pictures of women parting their labia to exhibit their genitals with feigned displays of ecstacy on their faces is not a true reflection of women's sexuality. Women do not typically act like this to enhance their own pleasure during sexual encounters. This is one of many examples of how pornography distorts female sexuality and misinforms viewers, many of whom learn about women and sex from this medium.

---

**Picture 50.** A naked woman is lying on her back with her legs open and stretched straight up into the air. Her head and arms are cut off by the bottom edge of the photograph. A muscular male construction worker dressed in hard hat and work clothes is shown operating an enormous jackhammer. He has placed its metal tip on the woman's vulva. Appearing in large letters at the top and the bottom of the photo is the quip,

> "At last. A simple cure for frigidity!" Source: *Slam* (reprinted in *Hustler,* July 1980, p. 52).

**Comment 50.** This sadistic joke reinforces the idea that aggression is an appropriate response to women who are sexually unresponsive to a man, or to men in general. The very concept of frigidity assumes that there is something severely wrong with women who don't find sex with a man or men satisfying. Not only is it heterosexist to assume that all women are heterosexual, but calling a woman frigid if she doesn't enjoy sex with a man presumes that the problem lies with *her,* not with the man with whom she is having sex. This is particularly unjustifiable in light of the fact that so many men are ignorant about female sexuality and preoccupied with satisfying their own sexual needs.

**Picture 51.** In a posed-looking "crotch shot," a staple image in pornography, a naked woman is lying on her back in the middle of a highway. Her arms are stretched above her head and her legs are wide apart, displaying her genitals for the viewer. Her face is not visible, and her breasts and torso are covered by a large white pillow. She is wearing the stiletto heels so popular in pornography. The caption accompanying this photograph refers to the woman as "our moving target." Source: *Penthouse,* December 1985.

**Comment 51.** Like most pornography, this photograph portrays the woman as a depersonalized, faceless sex object. The description of her as "our moving target" is also depersonalizing. Ironically, the picture shows the woman as immobilized and passive—an inert target, not a moving one. Referring to her as "our" moving target suggests she is owned by *Penthouse* and the male reader. This phrase is also an invitation to attack. Her high-heeled shoes add to her immobility. Perhaps such shoes are so favored in pornographic pictures because they severely restrict women's capacity to run, and hence to escape and to defend themselves.

---

**Picture 52.** A close-up of a woman's buttocks, the slit covered by a lacy G-string and a round target covering her vaginal opening, is the dominant focus of this photograph. The woman's torso and face are a mere background blur, contributing to her sexual objectification. Source: ?*Gallery,* 1984.

**Comment 52.** This woman is portrayed as *wanting* her vagina to be a target:

> "Think you can hit the bulls eye?" she asks. With what, one wonders? A bullet? A dart? "If you can [hit the bulls eye]," the fantasy woman goes on to say, "I might let you fuck me till we both drop from exhaustion."

This gross misrepresentation of female sexuality and behavior brings to mind one of the early slogans of the feminist anti-pornography movement:

"Pornography tells lies about women." The women invented by pornographers to turn men on usually have little in common with real women.

---

**Picture 53.** An attractive naked woman is lying on her back on a satin sheet in a very sensual photograph, her hair tousled, her painted mouth open and moist, conveying an impression of intense desire. Most of her pubic hair has been removed. Around her waist she wears a cartridge belt filled with bullets pointing toward her vagina. A thick leather harness runs from her neck to the cartridge belt and across her collarbone, suggesting that the woman is into sadomasochistic sex. The photo-frame is sliced off directly below her vagina, leaving her legless. Source: *Playboy,* January 1985.

**Comment 53.** Despite the fact that the woman in this picture is wearing bullets around her waist, she is portrayed as vulnerable rather than threatening. The bullets, which are phallic symbols, are pointing toward her vulva. Associating bullets with the body of a beautiful, aroused naked woman eroticizes them and, by extension, guns and violence. This dangerous association is further reinforced by the woman's sadomasochistic outfit.

---

**Picture 54.** In this photograph, a fully dressed man in the costume of a 17th-century courtier is shown holding a sword against the naked buttocks of a woman who is bent over a table. One of his hands is cupped over her right buttock as if he is about to spank her behind with the flat of his sword, or perhaps skewer it with the blade. Source: *Penthouse,* June 1986.

**Comment 54.** This photograph, like so many others in pornography, eroticizes male sexual violence toward women. The man's violence in this case appears to be in the guise of disciplining the woman. His aristocratic costume makes the scene look elegant and makes his action appear more acceptable (due to classism), while it also recreates the historical ambience of the Marquis de Sade.

Women in pornography are often naked while men are partially or fully clothed, as in this picture. This is but one of many manifestations of the gender inequality that characterizes pornography.

---

**Picture 55.** This photo shows a woman lying naked with her legs spread wide apart atop a counter in a gun shop. A man stands behind the counter, one hand grasping the woman's left breast as he licks it. His other hand holds her labia apart to enhance the graphic display of her vulva for the viewer. The woman is holding and caressing a pistol. Her eyes are closed, her lips apart, as if sexually aroused. The caption has the woman saying to the man:

> "Now shove that thing [the gun] in me and fuck my pussy with it until I come all over the tip." Source: *Stag*.

**Comment 55.** The depiction of a woman as wanting to be penetrated by a gun as if women would find this a sexually gratifying experience, is false and treacherous. Eroticizing weapons by associating them with attractive nude women in a state of sexual arousal is also very dangerous. The merging of sexual and violent images in pornography teaches men to connect sex with violence in real life. Since what is happening in pornography both reflects and influences what happens in real life, we should not be surprised to learn that some males do shove weapons up women's vaginas.

---

**Picture 56.** "Love and Kisses" is the incongruous imprint on the T-shirt of a woman whose shirt is being ripped off by multiple, anonymous hands on this record album cover. The hands grope at her, exposing her torso and one of her breasts. Her face is cut off by the photo-frame, depersonalizing her and transforming her into "any woman" for the viewer. Although rape is not overtly shown on this record cover, the picture conveys the impression of a gang rape about to happen. Source: Record album cover for *Love and Kisses*.

**Comment 56.** The association of the words *love* and *kisses* with the violent way in which the woman's shirt is being ripped and her body grabbed at exemplifies once again the dangerous merging of sex and violence so rampant in pornography.

---

**Picture 57.** An angry-looking man is roughly grabbing the breasts of a woman who is lying across his lap in this photograph. She is naked but for a garter belt and stockings. Her eyes are closed and she is smiling. The caption accompanying this picture reads:

> Let's face it, guys, some women are just begging for rough treatment. They whine, they nag, they sass you back when you give them an order. There's just one thing to do—give them what they deserve!

The woman appears to be unaware of the "rough treatment" in store for her. Source: *Take That Bitch!,* Vol. 1, No. 1 (Wilmington, Delaware: Eros Publishing Company), 1983.

**Comment 57.** The message here goes beyond merely giving men permission to beat and rape women; it explicitly *advocates* violence against women while placing the responsibility for this on women ("some women are just begging for rough treatment").

---

**Picture 58.** This is a close-up photo of the face of an enraged man harshly biting a woman's bottom. Source: *Take That Bitch!,* Vol. 1, No. 1, 1983.

**Comment 58.** Pictures like this condone the sexualization of male aggression as well as the acting out of this aggression on women's bodies. The contempt and hatred toward women revealed in both this picture and the magazine title are all the more striking when one remembers that these images were designed to excite men sexually.

---

**Picture 59.** The naked woman in this photo is on her hands and knees doggy-style, exposing her bottom, anus, and abundant pubic hair to the viewer. A nude man is holding a whip over her vaginal opening with one hand, and a burning cigarette close to her anus with the other. Welts or bruises are evident on the upper portion of one of the woman's thighs. This photo shows no faces, merely the thighs and buttocks of the woman, and the upper thighs, dangling penis, and hands of the man. The title of the magazine indicates that the woman in this picture is Asian. Source: *Cherry Blossoms,* No. 3, March 1977.

**Comment 59.** Although this photograph does not show the woman actually being burned or whipped, the presence and placement of the whip and burning cigarette invite viewers to use these weapons in their sexual fantasies and/or their overt behavior. The omission of faces in this photo serves to depersonalize both the man and the woman, facilitating the disinhibition of male viewers' sexual imaginations and their identification with the aggressor. But burning women does not remain a fantasy for some men and women. Some women's bodies have been burned with cigarettes in the course of sex torture by men engaged in pornographic enactments as well as by men who have been inspired or disinhibited by pornography.

---

**Picture 60.** This photo shows the head and upper torso of a naked woman, a breast exposed, leaning over and clutching a toilet bowl. An unseen hand above her head appears to be pulling a handful of her long wet hair upwards. The rest of her hair covers half of her face and drips on her back and shoulders and into the toilet bowl. Her mouth is wide open as she gasps for air, and a look of shock is visible on her face. Source: *Hustler,* February 1981.

**Comment 60.** This picture is the last in a series called "Dream Lover." At the beginning of the series, the woman is brutally beaten by her "dream man." The text informs us that the woman "senses the erotic nature of the humiliation which he [her lover] subjects her to." Translation: The woman realizes that her sexual partner has become sexually aroused by humiliating her. After being dragged by her hair to the bathroom, the woman's so-called dream lover experience climaxes in the scene described above in which she gasps for air after he has forcibly submerged her head in a toilet bowl. By choosing "dream lover" as the title for this story about a woman's torture, *Hustler* magazine once again reinforces the notion that women are turned on by torture.

---

**Picture 61.** Titled "Rating Guide," this photograph is a clip from a pornographic movie called *Girls USA*. A naked African American woman is clenching her teeth and grimacing in pain in this photo as a man pulls at a pair of clamps that are firmly attached to her left nipple. The man, fully clothed and wearing a tie, has a totally neutral facial expression. Source: *Hustler*, June 1981, p. 29.

**Comment 61.** *Hustler*'s film critic, who evaluates movies according to the stiffness of the erection they can be expected to produce, rated this film as ¾ erect. This means that he thought it was, "Worthwhile. Almost gets it up." He rejected the more positive "erection" option because that would have required the movie to be "a constant turn on." The quip that follows this maximally positive review category is: "If this [movie] won't get it up, you may be dead."

Most males feel entitled to rate women's bodies on a routine basis, as well as to inform them about what body parts they particularly like or dislike. Many of these males are angry and bewildered by the growing recognition that such verbal behavior, including apparently complimentary evaluations, are illegal forms of sexual harassment when uttered in the workplace.

---

**Picture 62.** The viewer of this photograph looks smack into the vulva of a naked woman who is leaning backwards on her elbows, with her legs spread wide apart. She is being tortured by a masked woman. Three clothespins are attached to her partially shaved genital area. Her torturer, who is clothed, is holding a knife to one of the victim's nipples with one hand, and pulling the hair on her head with the other. The victim's eyes are closed and her mouth is wide open, conveying that she is screaming. However, there is a staged quality about this photo that undercuts its authenticity. Source: *Cherry Blossom*, No. 3, March 1977.

**Comment 62.** Once again, the pornographers who orchestrated and photographed this picture have eroticized the torture of a woman. This time it is designed for viewers who get off on the idea or the reality of a woman being tortured by another woman. Even though the scenario appears to be staged, the physical pain for the victim, whose genitals and surrounding areas are being pinched by clothespins, must be real. It usually requires extended periods of posing to obtain publishable photographs.

---

**Picture 63.** A dishevelled woman is half sitting, half lying on the ground, her head lolling backwards, her mouth open in an expression of anguish on this Guns 'N Roses record cover. Her panties have been pulled down to her calves, her blouse is open exposing her breasts, one shoe is off—strongly intimating that she has been raped. Written in gigantic letters above her are the words, "GUNS N ROSES WAS HERE," further suggesting that the members of this rock band were responsible for raping her. Source: Guns 'N Roses record album cover.

**Comment 63.** The announcement that "GUNS N ROSES WAS HERE" sounds like a boast by this misogynist band of male musicians. The impression that these young men have raped a woman normalizes this misogynist crime on a mass media commodity purchased primarily by young men and women. One wonders how many girls and women were raped as a result of this blatant example of locker-room machismo. Given the band's hateful boast, my guess is that they themselves are likely to have engaged in rape.

---

**Picture 64.** This photo shows four hip-looking men wearing beads, long hair, and knee-high boots restraining a screaming woman clothed only in the stockings, garter belt, high heels uniform of pornography. The woman is squatting on the ground with her legs spread wide open to display her genitals to the viewer while the men hold her arms up and behind her head. One of the men is holding an open pair of scissors around one of the woman's breasts as if he is about to slice it. Source unknown.

**Comment 64.** The depiction of four hip-looking men engaged in violently abusing a woman lends legitimacy to the torture portrayed and implies that this behavior is also acceptable, even hip. The reader needs to keep recalling that pornographers create or select pictures they consider to be exciting masturbatory material for men. If men don't like the porn, it doesn't sell. It follows that some men are likely to be sexually turned on by this portrayal of a man about to cut a woman's breast. And, assuming that my theory (to be described in Part 3) is correct, more men will become sexually aroused by this idea or act on it after viewing this and similar depictions.

---

**Picture 65.** This is the cover picture of a hard-core porn magazine titled *Take That Bitch!* It shows a woman in lacy lingerie uncomfortably curled up on top of a high, narrow table with her head thrust back and her mouth gaping open. A masked man with a naked torso is clutching his erect penis an inch or so from her head, as he gazes at her in a threatening manner. One blurb on the cover announces,

> Over 150 Photos of Bitches Getting Belted!!!

Another proclaims:

> Orgasms Gush as Babes Bare Bottoms are Beaten! Source: *Take That Bitch!,* Vol. 1, No. 1, 1983.

**Comment 65.** The ridiculousness of the title's alliteration notwithstanding, the producer of this magazine makes it clear that his product is designed for men who are turned on by pictures of woman beating. The problem of woman beating/battering is extremely serious in the United States as well as in other countries. There is a growing attempt to address and remedy this form of woman abuse in some societies. Such efforts are seriously undermined by the pornography industry, which depicts such violence as sexually exciting, trivializes its harmful effects, and contributes to its normalization. The assumption of *Take That Bitch!* and pornography in general seems to be that whatever it takes to stimulate men's orgasms is okay because sex is okay, and only repressive anti-sex puritans would believe otherwise.

**Picture 66.** This picture is one in a sequence titled "Dirty Pool." The first picture in this series depicts a miniskirted waitress being pinched by a lecherous male pool player. The picture shown here features a naked woman sprawled on her back across a pool table and straddled by a muscular man dressed only in his waistcoat. The woman, seemingly aroused and excited, is moaning with pleasure and lifting her breasts to stimulate the man's penis, which he has placed between them. A second man is shown hazily in the background licking some indiscernible part of the woman's lower body. The text reads:

> Watching the muscular young men at play is too much for the excitable young waitress. Though she pretends to ignore them, these men know when they see an easy lay. She is thrown on the felt table, and one manly hand after another probes her private areas. Completely vulnerable, she feels one after another enter her fiercely. As the three violators explode in a shower of climaxes, she comes to a shuddering orgasm. . . . Source: *Hustler,* January 1983.

**Comment 66.** Some readers may be wondering if the "Dirty Pool" sequence is about gang rape or consenting sex. Pornographers love to blur this distinction. The depiction of initially reluctant women becoming turned on during a rape attack and orgasmic by the end of it is one of the most popular scenarios in pornography. And yes, it *is* rape—even if the woman *does* get turned on (an occurrence that is exceedingly rare, however). Being subjected to sex against one's will is rape. It is not the response of the attacked person's body that defines rape. If it were, many of the sexual encounters that are consented to but that turn out to be unpleasant and unsatisfying might be considered rape.

"Dirty Pool" was published about 2 months before the highly publicized gang rape of a woman in a bar in New Bedford, Massachusetts. Many male onlookers in that case applauded as the woman was raped. Might Larry Flynt, the owner of *Hustler* magazine, be considered partially responsible for this rape? Answering this question would require knowing about the rapists' and onlookers' familiarity with the "Dirty Pool" sequence in *Hustler* and its impact on them. There is no doubt that he *may* be partially responsible.

**Picture 67.** "Greetings from New Bedford, Mass." These words are printed in big letters in the format of a typical vacation spot greeting card. A naked, smiling woman, who is lying on her side on a pool table, is pictured below the friendly greeting. She is holding a pool cue with one hand and waving amiably with the other. New Bedford is described at the bottom of the card as:

> "The Portuguese Gang-rape Capital of America." Source: *Hustler,* August 1983.

**Comment 67.** This picture was published after the New Bedford pool table gang rape. Along with insulting and mocking this particular rape survivor, who was eventually hounded out of town after her rapists were found guilty in a court of law, this picture trivializes rape in general by joking about it. Surely the publication of this picture by *Hustler* magazine qualifies as defamatory toward the rape survivor, as an invasion of her privacy, and as sexual harassment.

---

**Picture 68.** *Hustler* magazine published a grotesque photo series depicting Gloria Steinem being viciously ravaged by a group of women. The photo selected from this sequence shows a pack of women aggressively clawing and biting "Gloria's" genital area. Blood from her genitals is smeared on the hands of two of the women attackers and around the mouth of one of them. An encapsulated photo in the upper left corner of the picture shows "Gloria," her nude breasts prominently displayed, screaming in terror as women restrain her by holding down her arms. The text in the upper right corner of this picture reads:

> Unable to menstruate after years of taking male hormones, Gloria is forced to bleed for her cause by the jagged teeth of the women she taught to hate. Source: *Hustler,* March 1984.

**Comment 68.** Many pornographers hate feminists and feminism with a passion. The viciousness of *Hustler* magazine owner Larry Flynt's attack on Gloria Steinem in this picture-cum-text may qualify him as the worst of them. He subjected Steinem to his misogynist venom on another occasion by publishing a photograph of her in *Hustler* on a "Most Wanted" poster for having urged people to engage in actions against pornography. Flynt declared that Steinem "should be considered armed with false propaganda and dangerous to the rights of all Americans." In reality, *Flynt* is the one who is armed with false propaganda and a menace to the rights, and lives, of all women.

In Flynt's diatribe accompanying the "Most Wanted" poster, he claims that pornography is "the healthy depiction of adult sexuality." The photographs described in this book show what a gigantic lie this is. This lie is further magnified by the fact that *Hustler* magazine has frequently published material that minimizes, legitimizes, and sexualizes the sexual abuse of children, particularly girls.

◆

**Picture 69.** Titled "The Cinch"—the name of a special kind of knot—this photograph of a page from a magazine provides instructions on how to tie up a woman properly and effectively. Five illustrative photographs show hands, feet, and wrists that have been carefully tied with rope. Excerpts from the accompanying text read as follows:

> As any experienced practitioner knows, a wrapping of rope is much easier to escape from than a wrapping which has been cinched. . . . If your object [*sic*] is in motion when the wrapping is being done, it may be quite difficult to cinch your knots. The cinches may be added after the main tying has been completed. This will ensure inescapable bondage as the photos on this page illustrate. . . . Next issue: A nonfiction photo essay on GAGS. Source: Master Mandrake (c/o ?.A.G.E. [the first letter of this acronym is missing], P.O. Box 26560, Los Angeles, California 90026).

**Comment 69.** There is nothing inherently wrong in learning how to tie knots that stay secure, but when this lesson is published in a pornographic or bondage magazine rather than a scout manual, it has frightening implications. Sadomasochists repeatedly insist that they believe in the infliction of pain and injury only with consent. If this were true, they should be more interested in how to tie knots from which people *can* escape than how to ensure inescapable bondage. But it would be ludicrous to believe that most sadists engage in their preferred sadistic acts only with masochists whose desires mirror their own.

To put it more bluntly: Many men who tie women up, beat them, skewer them, rape them, and/or mutilate them couldn't care less about their consent. Hence, the more inescapable the bondage, the more dangerous is the woman's plight. Note the use in the text of the term *object* to apply to a person as well as the possessive word *your* that precedes it ("if your object is in motion"). Such depersonalization increases the risk of abuse to the person or persons who have been depersonalized.

---

**Picture 70.** A naked woman in stiletto heels, her ankles and wrists bound tightly together with rope, is shown lying uncomfortably on her back on a carpet. Her head is on a pillow and her back is arched. Subdued lighting contributes to the glamorization of this woman's predicament. Source: *Penthouse,* June 1977.

**Comment 70.** This picture is the first of a series in a photo-essay titled "Bound for Glory" in which abduction, bondage, and imminent rape and murder are depicted as titillating, glamorous, fashionable, and upper-class. The text reads:

> Once upon a time a successful seduction occurred only after a long candlelit dinner. . . . No longer! Today's man wants his satisfaction, and he wants it now! Today's woman, however, still has romantic notions in her pretty little head, feminism notwithstanding. She still expects her cigarettes and her inner fires lighted. Fortunately there is a solution to this dilemma—Bondage. Simply tie her up!

This photo-essay reveals *Penthouse* magazine owner Bob Guccione's angry response to the women's liberation movement in the late 1970s. The author of the text claims that feminism has failed to change women's desires for romance and sexist conventions like men lighting their cigarettes. On the other hand, he maintains, *men* have changed; they have liberated themselves from their old ways and are no longer willing to take the time to court women in order to win women's sexual cooperation. They will simply tie women up and rape them.

The truth is that women have changed far more than men since the second wave of feminism erupted on the American scene in the early 1960s. Many men have responded to women's growing assertiveness by beating women up, raping them, torturing and killing them, and turning to children to satisfy their desire for power and adoration. Blatant reactionary political statements like those articulated in "Bound for Glory" clarify an increasingly important goal of pornographers in recent years—aside from ejaculation production: using penis power to try to fight women's liberation, and urging their consumers to do the same. Pornography reflects the backlash against feminism while also fueling it.

---

**Picture 71.** The cover of a magazine called *Bondage Love* displays an African American woman whose blouse is unbuttoned to reveal her breasts, and whose arms are tied to a curtain rod above her head. She appears to be aroused—her eyes closed, her mouth open, her head thrust backward—as a fully clothed man holds her around her waist and appears to be penetrating her. The victim-blaming message on this cover reads,

> Cock teasing was her titillating game—his method took care of such cunts . . . or did it? Source: *Bondage Love*.

**Comment 71.** While the title of this magazine combines the concepts of love and bondage, there is no sign of love in the picture or the caption. The words are blatantly contemptuous of women, referring to women whom men perceive as teases as "cunts," and implying that such women should be tied up and raped if they refuse to have sex. The implication is that women have no right to say no to men with whom they have flirted.

It is not possible to tell from the photo whether rape or intercourse is being depicted. The caption, however, suggests rape. Hence, this photo, like many of the pornographic cartoons presented earlier, reinforces the damaging myth that women enjoy being raped.

---

**Picture 72.** In an ad for *Oui* magazine, a long-haired adolescent girl with a sulky yet seductive expression on her face is sitting on a bed naked except for stockings. One small breast is visible above the metal bedstead. Her legs are wide apart but her genitals are hidden by her handcuffed wrists. The text of the ad reads:

> *How one family solved its discipline problem.*

Lately, Jane has been very, very naughty. That's why, in the current issue of *OUI* magazine, Jane is pictured in a variety of poses that restrict her movement. . . . So you see, it's for her own good. And not incidentally, your pleasure. Source: *Playboy,* August 1975.

**Comment 72.** This ad informs potential consumers that *Oui* magazine will provide them with pictures of a nude adolescent girl in a variety of suggestive bondage poses, thereby eroticizing incestuous bondage masquerading as parental discipline. The ad also makes it clear that consumers are expected to find these pictures pleasurable (read, "enjoyable masturbatory material"). Note *Oui*'s use of the phrase "restrict her movement" instead of the more blatant term "bondage." Perhaps *Oui*'s owner doesn't want it to be too obvious that he publishes child pornography.

---

**Picture 73.** This photo shows a woman's naked midsection (from the top of her breasts to just below her completely shaved genitals) adorned with studded leather belts and chains. A chain attached to a tight leather belt at the woman's waist is connected to a ring that pierces her labia minora. The woman's long painted nails clutch her stomach so tightly that blood drips from the punctured skin. The nails on her other hand dig into the flesh surrounding one of her breasts. The photographer has succeeded in making this pornographic picture look like an interesting and glamorous work of art. Source: *Hustler,* March 1984.

**Comment 73.** This picture of an objectified headless and legless woman gives the impression that the bondage paraphernalia on her body is merely decorative when, in reality, such gear is often used to hurt or torture women. By eroticizing the torture apparel and portraying the woman as enjoying pain (by wounding herself with her nails), this picture serves subtly to condone and glamorize the torture of women. The merger of art with pornography in this photo masks the violence.

---

**Picture 74.** A woman wearing only high stiletto heels is shown in a photograph gagged, bound, and hanging upside down in a fetal position. The rope wrapped around her waist appears to be suspended from the ceiling. Her left side faces the viewer, enabling him or her to see one of her breasts, an arm bound behind her back, and a large piece of tape plastered over her mouth. It is evident that the ropes have been tied very expertly and methodically (they have been cinched!), and that the woman is entirely incapacitated. Source: *Simone Devon,* No. 2 (Van Nuys, California: London Enterprises), August 1990.

**Comment 74.** *Simone Devon* magazine describes itself as "celebrating the psychological power of the bound beauty whose love bondage is as much for her pleasure as ours." This inane, self-serving nonsense is an attempt to deceive viewers into believing that the bound woman has not been rendered powerless. And since when do pornographers care whether or not the women they exploit find their work pleasurable? Clearly, this magazine is trying to appeal to men who want to believe this kind of rubbish.

This magazine is also geared for upwardly mobile, "respectable" men. The settings of many of the pictures are in elegant homes with lawns and gardens to convey an impression of "gracious living." The woman in this picture, who is referred to as Stefanie, is described as the "attractive star" of "the most strikingly visual bondage videos we've ever seen!" According to the text, Stefanie "masterminded the video herself, planning the picturesque settings, imaginative lighting, and the strict bondage positions as an expression of her own personal vision of sensual restraint."

Pornographers love to portray the women they use in pornography as willing and responsible for the ways they are posed. Sometimes they *are* willing and responsible (consider Madonna's poses in her book, *Sex* [1992], for example), but more often they are not. Certainly, it would be naive to trust pornographers' claims on this subject.

---

**Picture 75.** A woman, naked but for a garter belt, stockings, and minute panties, is kneeling on the floor in this picture as a fully clothed man binds her with rope. The man, whose face is barely visible, appears to be tightening her bonds as the woman, who is gagged, lovingly gazes at him. The ropes are concentrated around her arms and upper torso, with one rope pressing on her nipples. The text below the picture reads:

> True love reveals itself in many ways. If a guy ties his girlfriend in an excruciating position for long, painful hours, it shows he cares enough to

> want her to be a better person for the experience. Most girls appreciate this attention! Source: ?*Take That Bitch!,* Vol. 1, No. 1, 1983.

**Comment 75.** The message here is that true heterosexual love can best be expressed by a man hurting the woman he loves. The more pain he can inflict on her, the more love he shows. She is supposed to be grateful for his taking up his precious time to try to improve her! The sexism in this picture-text combination is very extreme, as it is in a great deal of pornography. If love is expressed by hurting the loved one, why doesn't a magazine like this also show a woman tying ropes around a naked man's penis and jerking it painfully from side to side? Why does it assume that the woman needs to be put through hours of agony in order to become a better person? The answer is obvious. Pornography is about eroticizing men having and exercising their power over women. This is why some feminists have correctly pointed out that pornography discriminates against women.

---

**Picture 76.** This picture is part of a series titled "Darkness at Noon." In it, a naked woman, whose arms appear to be severed just below her shoulders, stands in front of a tall phallic object in a scenic outdoor setting. The phallic object, which towers above the woman, is covered in black plastic with rope wrapped around it. The woman's head is also totally encased in black plastic and her legs are cut off by the bottom frame of the picture. The phallic object appears to have been especially constructed for this picture by a pornographer with artistic pretensions. Source: *Penthouse,* August 1983.

**Comment 76.** The woman in this picture has been depersonalized by her faceless, legless, and armless appearance. Dehumanizing individuals makes it easier to mistreat them. Throughout most of the "Darkness at Noon" series, women are photographed in various states of bondage. The text includes a few quotations from the sadistic, femicidal, pornographic classic, *The Story of O*. One passage reads as follows:

> First make sure to brand me with your mark . . . let the whole world know I am yours. As long as I am beaten and ravished on your behalf, I am naught but the thought of you, the desire of you, the obsession of you. That, I believe, is what you wanted. Well, I love you and that is what I want too.

Despite the deviousness of hiding behind arty quotations from a classic in which the main woman character embraces being tortured, *Penthouse* magazine owner Bob Guccione here gives his blessing to the torture of women for men's entertainment. Indeed, this photo-essay sexualizes torture and makes it appear desirable to some women.

---

**Picture 77.** The main picture on the cover of a bondage magazine called *Kane Photo Exchange* shows a clothed woman whose body below her neck is wrapped in transparent plastic held in place with tape. She is totally immobilized, her arms pinned to her sides by the plastic wrap. She is also gagged, and her head and eyes are covered by a tight-fitting cap, obliterating her vision. Only her nose is exposed to enable her to breathe. Three smaller pictures display women in other kinds of bondage apparel. The words "Rubber and Rope Specialists" are printed in large letters on the cover page, along with an announcement that the magazine is "Entertainment for Adults Only." Source: *Kane Photo Exchange,* No. 8 (Providence, Rhode Island), 1988.

**Comment 77.** The publisher of *Kane Photo Exchange* announces that he welcomes the magazine's readers' "amateur photos, nonfictional texts, props, and devises." There is no attempt to glamorize the women in these pictures. The focus is on the bondage equipment and how effectively it can enhance men's control over women. Stimulating creative ideas about the many different ways that women can be immobilized appears to be another of the magazine owner's objectives.

This issue of the magazine also includes order forms for other magazines such as *Spanked Employees, Foot Worship,* and *Wet Letter*—an enema magazine showing women whose "thirsty behinds crave soapy quarts . . . spreading wide in anticipation."

---

**Picture 78.** Another photograph from *Kane Photo Exchange* features a woman wearing heels, black lacy bra, and garter belt lying stiffly in a total state of immobility on what looks like a hospital gurney. An elaborate set of ropes confine her arms and legs and cut painfully into her shaved vulva. Since the viewer cannot see the woman's head, a small photo is inserted showing her sitting in her bondage gear. She is wearing a ball gag that forces her mouth to remain open and prevents her from speaking. A white cap covers her head and eyes. Source: *Kane Photo Exchange,* No. 8 (Providence, Rhode Island), 1988.

**Comment 78.** Although this woman's vulva is exposed, the rope that cuts into and separates her labia majora would make it impossible for a man to penetrate her in this bondage outfit. While some bondage costumes optimize access to women's orifices, others, like the one shown here, make them inaccessible. Whether or not men who prefer bondage gear that limits or prevents penetration are more interested in controlling women than obtaining sexual gratification, I do not know.

---

**Pictures 79 and 80.** Picture 79 shows three shots of the same woman. In the first, she is standing on a stairway that appears to be located in a butcher shop basement (a meat hook is hanging in the background). She is wearing a bra, a corset, stockings, and a ball gag. Ropes cut across her chest, torso, genital area, and legs, while her wrists are handcuffed and her arms stretched up above her head. The next shot shows a close-up of the woman's face with a very large ball gag in her mouth and a cap pulled down over her head to eye level. In the third, the cap is pulled over the woman's eyes and close to the end of her nose.

The same woman is used to model progressively more restrictive bondage gear in the four shots printed in Picture 80. In addition to the rope, cap, and ball gag described in Picture 79, the two photos at the top of Picture 80 show a back and front view of this woman with her arms tightly tied to her sides. In the lower two photos, she is wrapped from her neck to her feet in black plastic held in place by rope. One can barely tell that a human being is inside this carefully wrapped and bound package, except that her nose and her cleavage are visible. Source: *Kane Photo Exchange,* No. 8 (Providence, Rhode Island), 1988.

**Comments 79 and 80.** Whereas some of the bondage gear in these pictures obliterates the woman's vision and prevents her from being able to speak, her sense of hearing is never impeded. Presumably, the consumers of bondage paraphernalia want their captives to be able to hear their masters' orders, insults, threats, and verbal attacks.

Clearly, women who are bound and gagged in the ways documented in the photos from *Kane Photo Exchange,* whether or not they consent to it, and whether or not it happens to them in the course of their work in the sex industry or in their private lives, are at the complete mercy of the people who are with them. These individuals are free to take advantage of the vulnerability and helplessness of women in these disabling outfits in whatever ways they please. Describing women in such apparel as "captives" is therefore no exaggeration.

In a society where from 30% to 60% of young college males admit there is some likelihood that they would rape or force sex acts on a woman if they could get away with it (this research will be described in Part 3 of this volume), bondage represents a considerable danger to women. Furthermore, negative consequences to males who exploit women in such situation are improbable. Women who are violated while in bondage, particularly if they consented to it, are unlikely to report such abuses to the police. Those who do report are unlikely to get a sympathetic hearing.

---

**Picture 81.** Three pictures of mostly naked women with rope tied tightly around their large breasts are featured on the cover of a magazine titled *Tit Torture Photos.* A blurb on the cover boasts that there are more than 200 such photos in the magazine, constituting "the biggest bonanza of boob bondage ever published!" One woman's breasts are being squeezed so tightly by the knotted rope that it seems likely that her blood circulation was affected. This woman also has a large ball gag in her mouth and wears a pained expression on her face. In another photo, a C-clamp is being fastened onto the nipple of a naked woman's bound breasts. Source: *Tit Torture Photos,* Vol. 1, No. 1.

**Comment 81.** "Tit torture" is a distinct genre in pornography. The notion that a woman's breasts can be tortured separately from the rest of her body is a male fantasy related to males' tendency to segment women into various body parts, for example, "tits, cunt, and ass." But breasts have enormous psychological meaning for women as well as men in American culture—as a signifier of gender identification, sexuality, self-image, and maternal role. Women subjected to male aggression and/or sadism directed at their breasts probably experience particular kinds of trauma based on the significance and meaning their breasts have for them.

◆

**Picture 82.** A naked African American woman seated in a chair and bound by ropes is being tortured in various ways in four separate photos on a page of a magazine titled *Chair Bondage*. In the first two pictures, the woman is screaming in pain as an anonymous hand pinches her left nipple with a kitchen tong. A C-clamp is attached to her cheek in a third picture. In the fourth photo, she is more heavily bound and appears to be unconscious as she slumps forward in the chair. Source: *Chair Bondage,* Vol. 1, No. 1.

**Comment 82.** Use of ordinary household items in these pictures teaches viewers that they, too, can easily perform such torture at home. These photos, as well as many of those already described and many of those to follow, constitute visual evidence of sexual abuse and degradation of women by pornographers.

◆

**Picture 83.** This picture shows a woman, naked save for thigh-high stockings and high heels, lying on her back on the floor in a fetal position. Leather straps bind her wrists to her ankles and her ankles to one another. Her mouth is gagged and a rope is wrapped around her head, face, and neck at least 12 times. A shirtless man kneeling beside her appears to be engrossed in pulling at her nipple with a pair of pliers. Since rope covers her eyes and face, her facial expression is hidden from the viewer. Source unknown.

**Comment 83.** No part of a woman's body appears to be exempt from some kind of bondage. In this photo, it is the woman's head that is most heavily bound. There was absolutely nothing the woman in this photograph could do to control how badly the man pinched her nipple. Since her mouth was bound shut, she could not even tell him if the pain was unbearable. Nor could she communicate with her eyes, as they too were covered. Pornographers have to keep inventing new ways to bind and humiliate women in order to keep consumers purchasing new copies of expensive magazines.

---

**Picture 84.** A distraught-looking naked woman is lying on her back with her genitals toward the viewer. She is grappling with a chain that is wrapped around her neck in an apparent effort to prevent being choked by it. It appears that this chain is being yanked by someone outside the picture frame. A man (only his hairy lower leg and booted foot are visible) is kicking the woman in her genitals. She has a large welt on one of her thighs and bruises on her stomach. Source: *Shackled,* Vol. 1, No. 1.

**Comment 84.** Although one cannot be sure that the woman's welt and bruises are real, it seems unlikely that most hard-core pornographers employ skilled makeup artists to fake such signs of injury. We also know from the testimony of women who have been used in pornography that many of them have been beaten, raped, and tortured in other ways in these situations (see *Public Hearings,* 1983; Russell, 1993b).

---

**Picture 85.** The first picture in a three-photo sequence shows a woman in bondage lying on her back, her legs spread apart, as an anonymous hand starts pulling off her panties. She looks helpless and very distressed (she is crying). The next photo shows her naked from the waist down as a hand pulls her panties down her legs. The final picture focuses on her face and hands. Her expression is one of utter despair and agony. Rape is implied in this series, but not shown. Source unknown.

**Comment 85.** There is no way of knowing whether or not this woman was actually raped when these photos were taken. Given the authentic appearance of her facial expressions, it is difficult to believe that she wasn't subjected to some kind of traumatic experience. Furthermore, women who aren't numbed out by prior abuse would likely feel degraded simply by having such photographs taken of them. But regardless of what this woman experienced that day, the aim of the pornographer was to get men sexually turned on by her distress and the rape implied.

Presumably, the anonymity of the victim's perpetrator in this and many other pornographic pictures facilitates male viewers' abilities to fantasize themselves in this role.

---

**Picture 86.** This is the first page of a 19-photo essay titled "Housewifes' [*sic*] Horror" that chronicles a man's breaking into the home of an unsuspecting housewife, torturing her with bondage equipment, then raping and sodomizing her. In the first of three photos, the woman is standing in her living room with her head turned toward the window, where a strange man is looking in at her. The next picture shows the man, who has now entered her home, standing behind her and grabbing her arms as she struggles to get away. In the third scene, the man has forced her onto a chair and is starting to tie her to it with her arms behind her back.

The woman is well but modestly dressed, and the setting is that of a tidy, comfortable, and nicely furnished middle-class home. An excerpt from the accompanying text reads:

> He liked what he saw when he peered through the window. He was inside before she knew what was going on. She was a housewife who needed action, and he gave her some. Source unknown.

**Comment 86.** An excerpt from the text at a later point in this lurid male fantasy reads as follows:

> There wasn't anything she wouldn't do if he put enough pressure on her. She didn't want to respond, but her juicy cunt gave her away. He knew she'd never tell—she liked it too much!

This photo-essay eroticizes—for males—the idea of breaking into the home of a strange woman, then raping and torturing her. Elaborate bondage equipment is used in some of these torture scenes. (How the man managed to carry all the equipment in through the window remains unclear.) Notice how the text implies that the woman wanted to be attacked, and despite the extremity of the violations to which she is subjected, she is portrayed as becoming sexually excited by them.

Male pornographers often imply that a sexually alive or frustrated woman will welcome or respond sexually to any man, no matter how degrading or violent his behavior. This myth provides another example of men's inability to understand that most women do not share men's desire for anonymous, impersonal sexual engagements.

---

**Picture 87.** In this photograph, a naked woman's hands are tied to a horizontal bar over her head causing her to lean back against a wall. Her rear end is in contact with a carpeted floor while her legs are spread wide apart and raised in the air in front of her. Her legs are secured in this position by her feet being tied to another horizontal bar about 2 feet above the floor. A man is lying on the floor in front of her, one hand clapped over her left breast, the other pushing an elongated object into her vagina. Distress is evident on her face. The accompanying text reads:

> She won't open her legs for you, will she? Now they're open, and she can't close them! Serves her right for all the times she teased you. Now you can do anything to her, and she can't resist! Source unknown.

Comment 87. According to the dangerous message in this picture-cum-text, when a man feels "teased" by a woman (i.e., when he fancies her but she doesn't fancy him, or when she doesn't want to acquiesce to the sex acts he wants to engage in), he is justified in tying her up and forcing sex acts on her.

"Pornography is about fantasy, not reality," according to one of the favorite clichés of those who defend pornography. But it's hardly a fantasy for the woman in this photograph, who had a foreign object shoved up her vagina. Although the men who view this picture cannot touch the woman in the photograph, they can imitate the acts shown in the picture and/or they can feel that it gives them permission to force sex on an unwilling woman who has "teased" them. Many consumers respond to pornography in both these ways—as will be documented in Part 3 of this book.

---

**Picture 88.** The first photo in this two-photo spread shows a close-up view of the face and naked torso of a woman with ropes around her arms and chest. She appears to be in a state of considerable distress and alarm as a man simultaneously pulls her long hair with both his hands while dangling his penis over her face. It looks as if the man is about to force her to perform fellatio.

The second close-up on the bottom half of the same picture is a frontal shot of the same woman's genital area. The man's hands are all that the viewer can see of him as he pulls the woman's labia apart and begins to insert an Italian wine jug into her vagina. Source unknown.

**Comment 88.** These two pictures portray imminent oral rape and vaginal rape with a foreign object. Whereas some consumers want rape victims to be depicted as enjoying the violation, there is also a large market for men who want to see the rape victims suffer. Whether or not the woman in these pictures was really about to be raped, we do not know. We *do* know that some men need pictures of forced sex to become sexually aroused.

---

**Picture 89.** This photograph appears in a magazine devoted to the torture of African American women. A naked African American woman is shown sitting in a chair in a kitchen with a stove in the background. Her arms and ankles are tied to the arms of the chair, forcing her body and legs into a pelvic-exam-like position that exposes her genitals and upper thighs. While she is thus immobilized, a fully clothed woman places the nozzle of a vacuum cleaner over her clitoris. The bound woman's eyes are closed and her mouth is open—whether in distress or pleasure is hard to discern. Source: *Black Tit and Body Torture,* Vol. 1, No. 1.

**Comment 89.** The use of a vacuum cleaner on the genitals of an African American woman may reflect the racist association of African American female sexuality with dirt.

Pornography that portrays women as the abusers might seem to undermine the charge that these materials are sexist. Although the reaction of consumers is likely to be affected by the gender of the abuser, placing women in this role does not necessarily reduce the misogyny of the material. Abusive pictures like this are no less abusive because a woman is shown operating the vacuum cleaner. Some men enjoy seeing women abuse each other, and some men get turned on by such depictions in pornography.

---

**Picture 90.** This is the second page of a two-page photo-essay. The woman to be victimized in this story is introduced on the first page in the following way:

> Sally hated waiting for the bus—she was a hot juicy young bitch who couldn't stand the boredom. She was always ready for a good time, especially if the good time was a rough one.

Two men then accost Sally and start feeling her genitals. In the first of three pictures on the second page, the two jean-clad men tie Sally spread-eagle to the four corners of a table top. She is naked except for thigh-high stockings, garter belt, and high heels. Her mouth is ajar and her eyes are closed as one of the men leans over and kisses her left nipple.

The next photo shows one man kissing Sally's neck while the other man kneels on the table top and reaches to unzip his pants. In the third photo, one man watches as his buddy mounts the woman and begins to penetrate her vaginally. His pants are pulled down just far enough for the viewer to see his bare buttocks. The caption that accompanies these photos reads:

> The two guys read her right—they knew there'd be no trouble with a bitch like her. She loved it and they knew it. Abuse City. Source unknown.

**Comment 90.** To meet the needs of men who are queasy about forcible rape, pornographers love to portray a kind of rape-with-consent. In this photo-essay, for example, Sally is depicted as enjoying "rough sex," enjoying being totally immobilized and helpless, and enjoying the sex acts to which the two men subjected her. Assuming one believes the men's version of this incident—typically, a very unwise practice—this would mean that Sally was not a victim of rape. On the other hand, the caption quoted above ends with the term "Abuse City." It seems that the message here is not so much that Sally enjoyed sex, but that she—and other women—enjoy being sexually abused. This is exactly what many men believe, particularly rapists. Even in the most violent gang rapes, the perpetrators often believe that the victims wanted it.

Although Sally was given a name, she was still depersonalized by the derogatory term *bitch.* Men find it easier to rape a woman if they see her as a bitch or a cunt or a broad. The double standard of nudity is once again exemplified in these photos. Only in the last picture does a man bare his behind.

---

**Pictures 91 through 93.** The first of three photos from a booklet titled *Rape 2* shows a naked woman tied to what looks like a reclining dentist's chair. Her arms are bound together at the wrists and strung up above her head. Her legs are spread wide apart and hang over the armrests to expose her genital area, and her feet are tied to the lower chair frame. A fully clothed man is pressing the button on a large container of red fluid, causing it to flow down a long plastic tube the man has inserted into the woman's vagina. The woman is screaming in terror.

In the second photo, the same woman is tied upside down with her buttocks and genital area sticking up in the air while her head hangs down at the level of the man's crotch. While she performs fellatio on him, the man, still fully clothed, appears preoccupied with holding a funnel that he has inserted into her vagina. This time it is the funnel that is filled with red liquid.

Excerpts from the text accompanying these photographs read:

> Once more a woman was utterly in his power. He felt an overwhelming urge to abuse the girl, to humiliate her as grossly as possible, to reduce her to a heap of shit. . . . A tortured scream tore the silence of the chamber. . . . This reddish liquid, which burned so terribly, filled her cunt with flames. . . . The effect of the liquid was roughly equivalent to the bites of a hundred ants. Ecstatically Karl exulted in the indescribable agonies of the girl. . . . She was totally burnt-out and had cracked up under the strain of the mental torture she had been subjected to. . . . He swelled with pride that he seemed to have broken her will completely. . . . She really was nothing but a bundle of agonized nerves, completely broken down, degraded and debased.

The third photo is a close-up of the woman's thighs and genital area, her legs still spread wide apart. A lighted cigarette protrudes from her vagina. The text for this photo reads:

> Karl, however, had much more in store for her. "Now I need a short pause," he said, leering at her, "then we can go on! . . . The break will just be long enough for a fag [cigarette]," he said. After putting a burning cigarette up her vagina, Karl tells her, "You can call me when it burns." Source: *Rape 2* (Copenhagen, Denmark).

**Comments 91 through 93.** These three photos were published in a booklet that I acquired in Copenhagen, Denmark, in 1974. The text of the story that accompanies the pictures is written in English and German. A label informs the reader in four languages that, "We send magazines, photos, books, films, etc. all over the world. Write to us and ask for our illustrated catalogue free of charge." The description "High Class Pornography" graces the cover.

The entire booklet is devoted to Karl's different methods of raping and torturing the same woman. Even if we presume that the woman consented to being photographed for this publication, this does not negate the abusive nature of the acts to which she was subjected, for example, the insertion of a tube, a funnel, and red liquid into her vagina.

Feminists pointed out long ago that rape is an expression of domination and hatred. The blatant misogynistic sadism in the text of this booklet confirms this point. The man seems intent on destroying the woman's mind and spirit. This so-called high-class pornography is a graphic example of sexual terrorism.

---

**Picture 94.** In one of three photos titled "Columbine Cuts Up," a naked young woman smiles alluringly at the viewer as she stabs herself in the vagina with a large knife. Blood is splattered across her stomach. This bloody act of self-mutilation does not wipe the smile off her face.

The second photo shows a close-up of Columbine excising part of her labia with scissors. The third photo shows a close-up of her cutting off one of her nipples. The text for these photos reads as follows:

> Columbine, who stars in an off-off-off Broadway Company has a penchant for the self-destructive and self-mutilative. . . . "I would much rather masturbate with a knife than a dildo," says Columbine. . . . "I guess because I've always had an inferiority complex, I think of myself as deserving to be stabbed and killed." Source: *Chic.*

**Comment 94.** Tragically, some women, particularly those who were subjected to very traumatic forms of incestuous abuse as children, do mutilate themselves (although they don't typically target their genitals). Making masturbatory material out of these gruesome symptoms of male abuse is grotesque. It is shocking to realize that some men find it sexually exciting to see pictures of a woman mutilating her vagina and breasts and to read that she feels she deserves to be stabbed and killed. Perhaps those with sadistic impulses toward women can feel freer to fantasize or act out these impulses if they believe that women really want to be hurt. Whether or not this is correct, the fact remains that femicide, the misogynist killing of women, is a very prevalent crime in the United States and elsewhere.

And many women, both those who are murdered by men and those who are not, are stabbed and mutilated by them.

---

**Picture 95.** A woman who is naked except for a pair of moccasin boots, has been photographed lying on her back on a blanket in a forest. She has spread her legs invitingly apart and is holding her labia open with her hands. She looks sexually aroused as a large grizzly bear licks her lower stomach. Source: *Hustler,* Vol. 1, 1984.

**Comment 95.** This photograph comes at the end of a 10-page photo-essay called "Danielle: the Bear Facts." The fact that the woman is clearly displaying her genitals for the viewer rather than masturbating for her own pleasure makes the photo appear particularly contrived. What, one wonders, was the woman really feeling as the grizzly bear licked her stomach?

The bear is in the photograph for men who get sexually excited by seeing women having sex with animals (bestiality). Although this picture does not show the woman actually having sex with the bear, many a male viewer may fantasize this transpiring. Or perhaps the novelty of seeing a grizzly bear in this context or contemplating the danger the woman was in does the trick for some men. If my assumption that the woman must have been in danger is correct, it follows that her life was placed at risk for men's sexual entertainment.

---

**Pictures 96 and 97.** The cover of a booklet titled *Animal Love* shows a photo of a naked woman leaning back on her elbows with her legs spread wide apart to display her vulva and anus. A pig next to her is penetrating her vagina with his penis. It is clear that this is not a simulated act since an inch or so of the pig's penis is visible as it enters her vagina. The woman is looking down with an expression of deep resignation and shame.

In the second photo, the nude woman is crouched over in a doggy-style sex position as an approximately 200-pound filthy-looking pig mounts her from behind. The woman is reaching back to insert the pig's penis into her vagina. Another pair of hands holds the pig's hindquarters either to steady it or to help position the pig to effect vaginal penetration. Source: *Animal Love.*

**Comments 96 and 97.** These two photos were published in a booklet that I acquired in Copenhagen, Denmark, in 1974. The entire booklet is devoted to sex acts between the woman and a pig. Other photos show the pig's snout and mouth in the woman's genitals and the woman giving the pig's penis an open-mouthed kiss.

Most of the pornography stores I visited in Copenhagen had a section devoted to women and animals engaged in sex acts. These stores were located in well-to-do sections of town frequented by many tourists. Pornography involving bestiality is not only abusive and degrading to women, but abusive of the animal as well. It is surprising that the animal rights movement hasn't taken up this issue yet.

### *Femicidal Pornography*

The next 16 photographs provide examples of pornography depicting sexual femicide (the misogynist killing of women by males for sexual gratification). Of all the kinds of power one person can wield over another, the ultimate is the power of life and death. In these pictures, the death, murder, and mutilation of women are eroticized.

**Picture 98.** This is a poster advertising the notorious 1979 film called *Snuff* in which a woman was tortured, mutilated, and killed. In the final scene, a man rips out a woman's uterus and holds it up in the air while he ejaculates. Some people claim that the violent scenes were simulated while others believe they were real.

The poster features a picture of a beautiful young naked woman, her head lolling backwards. The picture has been cut into four pieces with a gigantic pair of bloody scissors displayed alongside the woman's body. Large quantities of blood are shown flowing from her neck, breasts, and upper pelvic region because these parts of her body were cut by the scissors. Three different blurbs add the final touch to this movie advertisement promising audiences an orgy of woman-hating violence:

> The picture they said could NEVER be shown. . . .
>
> The film that could only be made in South America . . . where life is CHEAP!

> The *bloodiest* thing that *ever* happened in front of a camera!! Source: Snuff Poster.

**Comment 98.** Even if we assume that the murder and mutilation portrayed in *Snuff* were simulated by trick photography, its fakery was apparently difficult to ascertain. The protests by feminists that greeted the opening of this 1979 movie caused the word *snuff* to become the generic term for pornographic films of sexual murders. In order for snuff movies to become a marketable underground genre in the pornography industry, a significant number of men must find it sexually arousing to watch the sexualized snuffing out of (mostly) women's lives. This is a terrifying and macabre reality for women in the United States, where so many have been killed or threatened by woman-hating strangers, colleagues at work, boyfriends, and husbands.

---

**Picture 99.** Featured in a picture called "Peaches 'n' Cream" is a pie tin containing what appears at first glance to be dessert. On closer inspection, the pie tin contains a fake severed breast topped by a large erect nipple and a smattering of cream. The text printed below the "dessert" reads as follows:

> A man who gets what he deserves is considered to have received his "just desserts." Here are a few sweet rewards as composed by photographer Steve Allison. One would be hard put to find a more delicious ending to any meal . . . or a lovelier stimulant to whet a rather different form of appetite. Source: *Gallery,* January 1980.

**Comment 99.** This picture is part of a series called "Just Desserts" in which women's breasts are depicted as various foods. Men are expected to find humorous the idea of women's breasts (only perfectly shaped ones, of course!) being cut off and served to men as food to reward them for . . . what exactly? For being members of the superior gender? The gruesomeness of these pictures is accentuated by the knowledge that some men do cut off women's breasts and decorate their corpses with them.

The publisher of *Gallery* magazine appears to have been so confident about the tastefulness of the "Just Desserts" series that these pictures were made available as posters. Presumably, they would be displayed in the purchasers' homes or offices, indicating that women (and children, if displayed in homes) were also expected to enjoy them. I doubt that men would find it equally funny and worthy of public display if the ingredients of the desserts had been severed penises and balls. As taboo as cannibalism is in the United States, it is not an uncommon feature in pornography, most examples of which portray women as food for men.

---

**Picture 100.** In this *Hustler* magazine cover picture, a woman has been placed head first into a manual meat grinder and is coming out the other end looking like ground beef. Her buttocks and legs, which are doused with sleek body oil, protrude gracefully from the top of the grinder. A mound of ground woman (head and upper body) has accumulated on a plate on a table under the meat grinder. A sign that resembles a meat packaging stamp proclaims, "Last all meat issue–Grade 'A' Pink." The following quote from Larry Flynt also graces the cover: "We will no longer hang women up like pieces of meat." Source: *Hustler,* June 1978.

**Comment 100.** Feminists have frequently protested that women in pornography are treated like pieces of meat. Larry Flynt used this charge as a pretext to escalate his assault on women. Although his taunt,

> We will no longer hang women up like pieces of meat,

sounds like an unexpected concession to feminists, the picture is announcing that he will grind women up—that is, kill them—instead. There is an obvious cannibalistic element in this piece of *Hustler* porn.

---

**Picture 101.** Inside *Hustler*'s woman-in-a-meat-grinder issue are two photos of naked women being served as meat dishes. The first photo shows a naked woman lying on her back between two hamburger buns. She is the meat patty, surrounded by onion, tomato, and lettuce. Catsup has been poured on her stomach, legs, and between her large breasts. She is holding her legs apart to display her vulva and pubic hair. An excerpt from the accompanying text reads,

> Grilled indoors or out, this pink patty takes two hands to handle.

The adjoining photo shows a headless and legless woman lying on her stomach—her buttocks facing the viewer—as the meat in a plate of spaghetti noodles. Sauce covers her back and behind. The viewer can see the woman's genitals, as she has reached her hands underneath her torso between her severed legs to hold her labia apart. Source: *Hustler,* June 1978.

**Comment 101.** Here Flynt carries the "woman as meat" joke further: He will no longer hang women up like pieces of meat, he will make meals out of them (cannibalism). These pictures, along with the cover picture, are graphic evidence of Flynt's crudity, misogyny, and violence.

Once again, cannibalism is implied in these two pictures. Some murderers, particularly male serial killers, do cook and/or eat parts of women, children, and sometimes men. A popular and highly acclaimed Hollywood movie, *The Silence of the Lambs,* featured such a cannibalistic serial killer.

---

**Picture 102.** This photo, published in an issue titled "The Best of *Hustler,*" shows a naked woman, head shaved and hands in cuffs, sitting on a chair with her legs straddled over the armrests, exposing her vulva. A uniformed male officer on her right side has one hand under her right leg while the other holds her head, turning her face toward him as he gazes intently into her blank face. A uniformed woman on the woman's left side is shaving off the naked woman's pubic hair with a razor and shaving cream. Source: *Hustler,* 1979.

**Comment 102.** This photograph is from a photo-story titled "The Naked and the Dead" about the fate of the woman in the picture just described. The woman is already naked in the first picture as she is led from a cell by fully clothed guards. In the second scene, she is shown having her head shaved—an act reminiscent of the shaving of inmates' heads in Nazi concentration camps. The picture described above comes next, followed by one in which the woman is raped by a male guard. The final picture is blank except for the word *POOF!* in large letters, suggesting that the woman was murdered.

For the umpteenth time, we have to think about what it means for the humiliation, rape, and murder of a woman to be considered entertaining for men, to be used by men as masturbation material, and to be judged by

Larry Flynt or one of his staff at *Hustler* as one of the magazine's best contributions. One wonders what the principal criterion was for choosing "The Best of *Hustler*." Was it pictures presumed to result in the maximum number of ejaculations?

---

**Picture 103.** A photo of a naked woman shows her standing in a Christ-like position with her arms outstretched and her head slumped to one side. Blood is splattered all over her body. Someone outside the picture frame is pulling the woman's left nipple with a pair of heavy pliers. The caption below the heading "SNUFF LIB" reads: "The incredible and mysterious saga of a film none of us will ever see. By *Cheri*'s resident master of gore." Source: *Cheri.*

**Comment 103.** The term *snuff lib* suggests that aspiring perpetrators of femicide have been oppressed by having to remain in the closet. It is also a call to men who would like to kill one or more women, or who already know they enjoy killing women, to come out of this closet to act out their murderous desires. Given all the serial killers of women that this culture has produced in the past 30 years, distributing pornography like this picture represents the height of irresponsibility. And how repulsive it is that *Cheri* magazine would have, or pretend to have, a "resident master of gore."

The meaning of the caption's statement that the photograph is from a film that "none of us will ever see," is unclear. Perhaps it signifies that no men (clearly "us" does not include women) will ever be able to see the film because—as a record of murder—it is too dangerous to distribute, even underground.

---

**Pictures 104 through 106.** These are 3 of 11 photographs from a photo-essay titled "Sakura" that appeared in *Penthouse* magazine. A haiku, a classic Japanese poetry form, accompanies the photos in an attempt to provide them with artistic credibility and to render their appeal to necrophilia more acceptable to middle-class consumers. Photographer Akira Ishigaki describes the meaning of the title as follows:

> *Sakura* is the word for the cherry blossom. From my childhood . . . I recall the resemblance between the petals of the cherry blossom and a woman's body. In the spring of my twelve years, I caressed the petals with my fingers, kissed them gently with my lips. Source: *Penthouse,* December 1984.

Ishigaki's sensitive and subtle verbiage contrasts dramatically with the brutal, femicidal photographs that eroticize the torture, bondage, hanging, and death of young Japanese women or girls (several look like teenagers). The implicit message of this series is that the portrayal of extreme brutality toward women and girls can be published in *Penthouse,* a soft-core magazine, when it meets society's artistic standards.

◆

**Picture 104.** The photograph on the title page of this photo-essay shows the naked rear view of a girl/woman, her shaved genitals visible, seemingly unconscious or dead and lying face down. Both legs are bent at the knees, and her left calf is twisted into an upright position by a taut rope, and tied at the ankle. Child-like little white socks cover her feet. Her splayed body is viewed against the background of a rocky, coastal bluff. Source: *Penthouse,* December 1984.

**Comment 104.** This picture conveys an aura of abduction—of a kidnapped young woman being taken to an isolated coastal area to be tortured and killed. The taut rope attached to the girl/woman's leg suggests an unseen captor, placing the male viewer in this role. The shaving of the girl/woman's pubic and leg hair contributes to the glamorization of her plight. Shaving re-creates the woman as child, increasing her vulnerability and, hence, her desirability. Imagine how hairy legs would de-eroticize this image for men.

◆

**Picture 105.** Once again, the main focus of this picture is on the naked buttocks and legs of a girl/woman who is lying face down, hands tied behind her back, her legs close together with the bare soles of her feet toward the viewer and her genitals partially exposed. Once again, the lifelessness of her body lying on a rocky cliff by the sea conveys the impression of a corpse. Source: *Penthouse,* December 1984.

**Comment 105.** There is an eerie lifelessness about this photograph. Ishigaki has used his skills to glamorize and eroticize the buttocks of a girl/woman's corpse. The effect is chilling and macabre; the frozen posture conveys the impression of rigor mortis. Pictures like this and the previous one eroticize necrophilia and/or intensify the erotic response to it in those males who are already sexually excited by this idea or practice.

---

**Picture 106.** This photograph shows a girl/woman in a harness, her arms bound behind her back, suspended from a tall tree by a rope that is tied to the harness. She is dressed in a long Japanese-looking outfit and short white socks, one leg exposed to her thigh. She is apparently dead or unconscious, her body limp, her head slumped forward. Around her are many tall trees with leafless branches. The photo's ambience is bleak and menacing. Source: *Penthouse,* December 1984.

**Comment 106.** This picture evokes recollections of the lynching of African Americans who, after being tortured and murdered, were typically left hanging from trees. Two months after this issue of *Penthouse* magazine appeared on the stands, Jean Kar-Har Fewel, an 8-year-old Chinese girl living in North Carolina, was found raped and murdered, tied to a tree with ropes around her neck. Many feminists believe that *Penthouse* magazine owner Bob Guccione is in part responsible for her horrifying death.

It is difficult to convey the curious, disembodied, and detached feeling of these three pictures of objectified female bodies adrift in timeless, depopulated landscapes. It is hard to believe that these girls/women ever existed except as shapeless, truncated forms. Ishigaki's delicate prose and technically beautiful photography contribute to making the vicious content of these pictures more acceptable, thereby serving to legitimize the violence against women and girls implied in these scenes.

---

**Picture 107.** This picture ad for a movie called *Maniac* shows the lower half of a rough-looking jean-clad man holding a large blood-tipped knife in one hand and the severed head of a woman in the other. There are pools and splatterings of blood everywhere. Both his knife and her head are being held at crotch level, drawing attention to the bulge in the man's pants. The following message is written graffiti-style on the ad:

I WARNED YOU NOT TO BE OUT TONIGHT

and signed

MANIAC. Source: Movie called *Maniac*.

**Comment 107.** *Maniac* warns women and girls that if they don't obey men, their lives are at risk. The message for *males* is that they are entitled to punish, perhaps even kill, females who don't obey their orders. Research shows that there are significant changes in males' attitudes toward females and rape after watching woman-slashing movies like *Maniac* (see Part 3). (The term *slasher* movie is generally used to describe this genre, but it is virtually always females who are being slashed; hence, use of the gender-specific phrase "woman slashing" is more appropriate.)

Although there is no nudity in this ad for *Maniac,* this genre of film invariably requires the female victims to expose their bodies and to engage in sexually suggestive poses and behavior as a prelude to the orgy of brutality that climaxes in their deaths. This combination of sex and violence serves to sexualize violence against females.

Although some people differentiate between woman-slashing movies and pornography, most of the former meet the definition of pornography presented in the introduction to this book. I believe that these simulated snuff films, which I refer to as soft-core snuff movies, sexualize femicide and other forms of violence against women and girls. Because these films have become very popular with young Americans, particularly young impressionable adolescent males, they are especially dangerous.

---

**Picture 108.** This horrendous picture of an old Japanese print from the late 14th century titled "Disembowelment" was republished in a Japanese magazine on sadomasochism. At the center of the picture is a very old woman draped in traditional attire, one breast exposed, seated on the floor. Her left hand is plunged into the vagina of a young woman who is standing beside her doubled over at the waist. The young woman is naked but for a flimsy cloth around her waist; her mouth is gagged, her torso is bound, and her overall appearance is one of extreme discomfort.

A second young nude woman in the foreground is lying on her back, her feet tied to a horizontal pole on the ground to keep her legs apart. Her arms and shoulders are bound, and her bloody innards are piled on top of her stomach and cascading to the floor beside her. Sitting cross-legged on a low table behind the old woman is a fully clothed smiling young man who is masturbating his oversized penis as he watches her at work.

This intricate picture illustrates an ancient Japanese folk tale. According to the text, the print depicts

> a celebrated occurrence of the time—rather similar to certain so-called "ritualistic" murders . . . of modern times. . . . According to the legend, a wealthy young reprobate, Shangi Kuto, . . . grew increasingly to have tastes which we would now call "de Sadian!" The story relates how he conferred a substantial amount of gold on one Hessuto Mofini, a withered old crone with a fervent hatred of young women, with the stipulation that she arrange some extravagant "entertainment" for him. The aged woman . . . drugs two young girls, trusses them up in her house and, while the young "playboy" watches (and masturbates) she disembowels them with a large, sharp knife . . . having earlier subjected them to various tortures, including the insertion of lighted candles into their respective vaginas.
>
> . . . The old woman and young Shangi Kuto suffer beheading and mutilation at the hands of starving dogs, after being tried before a celebrated judge. . . . (All quotation marks in the original.) Source: Print "*A Garden of Pain*" (Japan).

**Comment 108.** I cannot recollect ever reading about a woman who mutilated and murdered other women for money in my research on femicide over the years. I have come across a few cases of women who have murdered and mutilated their abusive husbands, but these kinds of female perpetrators are very rare compared with the numbers of men who have engaged in mutilation murders—of both males and females. Jack the Ripper is perhaps the most notorious (or celebrated) example of such a serial killer.

It is worth noting that at least the Japanese folktale makes it clear that the old woman does not represent women in general (she is described as having "a fervent hatred of young women"). The painful fate of the old woman and young playboy described in the folktale sets it apart from most Western pornography in which the rapists and other perpetrators typically go unpunished. The failure to portray negative consequences to men who hurt women in pornography contributes to its destructive impact on men (to be explained in Part 3).

---

**Picture 109.** This line drawing of a gory femicidal torture scene in what appears to be an outdoor setting is another 14th-century Japanese print that was reissued in *A Garden of Pain.* With his left hand, a balding, middle-aged man has shoved a long curved sword so far up a naked woman's vagina that it has exited through her stomach. With his right hand, this man, wearing a robe and a smile on his face, is using a plier-type instrument to tear off the woman's right nipple. The woman's body is arched backwards, her neck is circled by rope, and her arms and a foot are tied to a pipe a few feet below her head forcing her legs wide apart. Long needles protrude from her neck. The tube of a small enema-like syringe has been stuck up her anus. Her right leg has been sliced from her ankle to her knee. It gapes open, revealing her flesh and muscle. Blood gushes from the hole in her chest where her nipple has been ripped off. Blood also trickles from her mouth and from the wounds on her neck, stomach, leg, and inside her vagina. With her eyes open and a blank expression on her face, it is not clear whether she is alive, unconscious, or dead.

Two mutilated women's corpses are hanging upside down from crosses in the background, their feet tied far apart. Blood and/or entrails falls from the vagina of one of these corpses. Various torture implements are on the ground within reach of the man, for example, long needles, scissors, rope, knives, and two small, jar-like containers. The woman's flowered robe lies on the ground nearby. Source: Print "*A Garden of Pain*" (Japan).

**Comment 109.** This depiction of a Japanese Jack-the-Ripper engaged in lethal and mutilating torture is the most gruesome picture I have ever seen. It seems doubtful that the artist could have created such a picture unless he suffered from a strong urge to torture, mutilate, and kill women. More important, however, is the issue of how such pornographic art affects its viewers. This question will be discussed in Part 3.

---

**Picture 110.** Four photographs of women's corpses (these pictures are not simulated) are lying on a background of what appears to be wrinkled human skin that has the texture of leather. Ten razor blades have been placed at the corners or edges of the photographs as if to attach them to the skin. A severed clitoris and nipple, as well as two unidentifiable pieces of female flesh, have been fastened to the skin with fish hooks and safety pins.

One photograph shows the decapitated corpse of a naked woman lying on her back, her bloody neck and shoulders facing the viewer. Her arms, from which the hands have been severed, are folded over her large breasts.

An aerial view of another woman's naked corpse is displayed in the second photograph. She is lying on her back on the floor, her right leg sharply bent, frog-like, with her heel touching her crotch. Her left leg is missing, her trunk is ripped open, her innards are falling out of her lower stomach and pelvic area, and her genitals have been decimated. A long knife is lying on top of clothes at her side, suggesting that this woman was murdered. A deep wound from her right shoulder to below her armpit has almost severed her arm. Flesh has been cut off around her right knee, exposing bone and muscle. There are stab wounds on her right breast and long cuts on her left thigh. She appears to have lost her right eye and blood is trickling from her nose.

The third photograph features another aerial view of a woman's naked corpse lying on her back on a bathroom floor next to a toilet. Her left arm is stretched above her head while her right arm is bent over her chest. Blood is splattered all over her body and on the floor.

The fourth and largest photograph shows the nude, severed trunk of a woman whose legs have been amputated at her knees. This truncated corpse is on its side, the thighs are closed, and the woman's pubic hair is plainly visible. There is a large bloody gash where the right thigh connects with the woman's torso. Aside from this, there is a peculiar absence of blood, suggesting that the corpse has been cleaned. Source: *Hustler,* June 1990, p. 8.

**Comment 110.** This picture, published by *Hustler* magazine in 1990, also ranks as one of the most barbaric I have ever seen. Why do so many men (*Hustler* magazine had a circulation rate of 808,667 paid subscribers in 1997) find the death, injury, mutilation, and murder of women represented by this picture so acceptable that those who saw it failed to generate a public outcry after this pornographic picture was published in *Hustler?* What would the reaction have been if a comparably sadistic picture targeted African American people and was published in a white right-wing publication? What if a comparably sadistic picture targeted gay men and was published in a heterosexual magazine? What if a comparably sadistic picture targeted men and was published in a women's magazine? I'll wager that the reaction would have been very different. But why? Why is violence against women, even the most extreme forms of it, still considered harmless entertainment for men by some of the world's most educated people?

## CONCLUSION

Rape, battery, and murder are typically considered criminal offenses, yet the portrayal of these crimes against women is a popular form of entertainment in many countries. Millions of males regularly ejaculate to degrading pictures of women. This in turn intensifies their sexual response to women being abused. It is this sexual component, including the sexual gratification involved, that sets pornography apart from nonpornographic depictions that are degrading and/or violent toward women, and that makes pornography particularly dangerous.

That it is considered acceptable to treat women in the ways photographed here implies more than a tolerance of, and desensitization to, women's pain and degradation. It constitutes a massive hate crime against women as a gender. Would males be so cavalier about pornography, labeling it as mere free speech, if, instead of the rape of women by men, pornography celebrated women cutting off men's penises and testicles? Societies that call themselves civilized cannot at the same time continue tolerating pornography's invitation to men to rape, abuse, mutilate, and kill women.

The following words of Dworkin and MacKinnon (1988, p. 61) are very apt here: "What would it say about one's status if the society permits one to be hung from trees and calls it entertainment—calls it what it is to those who enjoy it, rather than what it is to those to whom it is done?"

## NOTES

1. Of course, there is nothing wrong with sexual excitement or sexual gratification per se. But there *is* a serious problem when these sensations are stimulated by

abusive images, including the objectification of women. This point will be addressed in greater depth in Part 3.

2. The term *femicide* refers to the misogynist killing of women by men (see Radford & Russell, 1992).

3. We cannot even begin to know what sexuality would be like in a truly egalitarian society. This also applies to lesbian relationships.

4. This statement is based on one of my research trips into the pornography district in San Francisco in 1995, and the viewing of Michelle Handelman's documentary film titled *Bloodsisters,* which celebrates the beliefs and practices of the lesbian sadomasochist community (see Russell, 1996b).

5. A question mark at the beginning of a source indicates uncertainty that it is correct. Several examples of the hard-core pornography included in this book were, like this one, published in the first issue of magazines (Vol. 1, No. 1). This is because many of them did not last more than one issue.

# PART III

# PORNOGRAPHY AS A CAUSE OF RAPE

---

The relationship between particularly sexually violent images in the media and subsequent aggression . . . is much stronger statistically than the relationship between smoking and lung cancer.

*Edward Donnerstein, 1983.*

## PORNOGRAPHY IS NO FANTASY

> I don't need studies and statistics to tell me that there is a relationship between pornography and real violence against women. My body remembers.
>
> *Woman's testimony, Public Hearings, 1983*[1]

> Before pornography became the pornographer's speech it was somebody's life.
>
> *Catharine MacKinnon, 1987, p. 179*

When addressing the question of whether or not pornography causes rape, as well as other forms of sexual assault and violence, many people fail to acknowledge that the actual *making* of pornography sometimes involves, or even requires, violence and sexual assault. Testimony by women and men involved in such activity provides numerous examples of this (*Attorney General's Commission,* 1986; *Public Hearings,* 1983).

In one case, a man who said he had participated in over a hundred pornographic movies testified at the Commission (1986) hearings in Los Angeles as follows:

> I, myself, have been on a couple of sets where the young ladies have been forced to do even anal sex scenes with a guy which [*sic*] is rather large and I have seen them crying in pain. (p. 773)

Another witness gave the following testimony at the same hearings in Los Angeles:

> Women and young girls were tortured and suffered permanent physical injuries to answer publisher demands for photographs depicting sadomasochistic abuse. When the torturer/photographer inquired of the publisher as to the types of depictions that would sell, the torturer/photographer was instructed to get similar existing publications and use the depiction therein for instruction. The torturer/ photographer followed the publisher's instructions, tortured women and girls accordingly, and then sold the photographs to the publisher. The photographs were

> included in magazines sold nationally in pornographic outlets. (Attorney General's Commission, 1986, pp. 787-788)

Peter Bogdanovich (1984) writes of *Playboy* "Playmate of the Year" Dorothy Stratten's response to her participation in a pornographic movie:

> A key sequence in "Galaxina" called for Dorothy to be spread-eagled against a cold water tower. The producers insisted she remain bound there for several hours, day and night. In one shot of the completed film, the tears she cries are real. (p. 59)

Although *Galaxina* was not made for the so-called adult movie houses, I consider it pornography because of its sexist and degrading combination of sexuality and bondage.

It should not be assumed that violence occurs only in the making of violent pornography. For example, although many people would classify the movie *Deep Throat* as nonviolent pornography because it does not portray rape or other violence, we now know from Linda (Lovelace) Marchiano's two books (*Ordeal* and *Out of Bondage;* Lovelace, 1981, 1986), as well as from her public testimony (e.g., *Public Hearings,* 1983), that this film is, in fact, a documentary of her rape from beginning to end.

Most people, including some of the foremost researchers on pornography in the United States, ignore the violence used by pornographers in the manufacturing of these misogynist materials (e.g., see Malamuth & Donnerstein, 1984). As Catharine MacKinnon (1987) points out in one of the opening epigraphs to this section, pornography is somebody's life before it becomes the pornographer's free speech (p. 179). Testimony presented at the hearings held on the antipornography civil rights ordinance in Minneapolis, Minnesota, in 1983 provides powerful evidence for the truth of her statement (*Public Hearings,* 1983; Russell, 1993b).

Before we can address the issue of pornography as a cause of rape, it is important to know the proclivities of those who read and view pornography. Hence, data on males' propensity to rape will be presented next.

## MALES' PROPENSITY TO RAPE[2]

---

> Why do I want to rape women? Because I am basically, as a male, a predator and all women look to men like prey. I

fantasize about the expression on a woman's face when I "capture" her and she realizes she cannot escape. It's like I won, I own her.

*Male respondent, quoted in Shere Hite, 1981, p. 718*

Research indicates that 25% to 30% of male college students in the United States and Canada admit that there is some likelihood they would rape a woman if they could get away with it.[3] In the first study of males' self-reported likelihood to rape that was conducted at the University of California at Los Angeles, the word *rape* was not used; instead, an account of rape (described below) was read to the male subjects, of whom 53% said there was some likelihood that they would behave in the same fashion as the man described in the story *if* they could be sure of getting away with it (Malamuth, Haber, & Feshbach, 1980). Without this assurance, only 17% said they might emulate the rapist's behavior. It is pertinent to know exactly what behavior these students said they might emulate:

> Bill soon caught up with Susan and offered to escort her to her car. Susan politely refused him. Bill was enraged by the rejection. "Who the hell does this bitch think she is, turning me down," Bill thought to himself as he reached into his pocket and took out a Swiss army knife. With his left hand he placed the knife at her throat. "If you try to get away, I'll cut you," said Bill. Susan nodded her head, her eyes wild with terror.
>
> The story then depicted the rape. There was a description of sexual acts with the victim continuously portrayed as clearly opposing the assault. (Malamuth et al., 1980, p. 124)

In another study, 356 male students were asked:

> If you could be assured that no one would know and that you could in no way be punished for engaging in the following acts, how likely, if at all, would you be to commit such acts? (Briere & Malamuth, 1983)

Among the sexual acts listed were the two of interest to these researchers: "forcing a female to do something she really didn't want to do" and "rape" (Briere & Malamuth, 1983). *Sixty percent of the sample indicated that under the right circumstances, there was some likelihood that they would rape, use force, or do both.*

Jacqueline Goodchilds and Gail Zellman (1984) conducted personal interviews with high school males and females between 14 and 18 years of age to find out under what circumstances they believed it to be "OK for a guy to hold a girl down and force her to have sexual intercourse" (p. 241). Seventy-nine percent of the study subjects thought it was acceptable to rape a girl in at least one of nine circumstances. The high school students rank ordered the different circumstances that justified the assaultive male behavior from the least justifying to the most justifying:

1. He spends a lot of money on her;
2. He's so turned on he can't stop;
3. She is stoned or drunk;
4. She has had sexual intercourse with other guys;
5. She lets him touch her above the waist;
6. She says she's going to have sex with him and then changes her mind;
7. They have dated a long time;
8. She's led him on;
9. She gets him sexually excited. (Goodchilds & Zellman, 1984, pp. 241-242)

Goodchilds and Zellman conclude that their experiment shows that their adolescent subjects

> accept as the norm an essentially adversarial cross-gender relationship by the man against the woman as an ever-present and sometimes acceptable possibility in the context of intimate cross-gender encounters. (p. 242)

To put it in plainer language: Both male and female adolescents see rape of females by males as an "ever-present and sometimes acceptable possibility" in women's lives.

Some people dismiss the findings from these studies as "merely attitudinal." However, this conclusion is incorrect. Malamuth has found that male subjects' self-reported likelihood of raping is correlated with physiological measures of sexual arousal to rape depictions. Clearly, erections cannot be considered attitudes.

More specifically, the male students who say they might rape a woman if they could get away with it are significantly more likely than other male students to be sexually aroused by portrayals of rape. Indeed, these males were more sexually aroused by depictions of rape than by mutually consenting depictions. In addition, when asked if they would find committing a rape sexually arousing, they said yes (Donnerstein, 1983, p. 7). They were also more likely than the other male subjects to admit to having used actual physical force to obtain sex with a woman. These latter data were self-reported, but because they refer to actual behavior, they too cannot be dismissed as merely attitudinal.

Looking at the sexual arousal data alone (as measured by penile tumescence) rather than its correlation with self-reported likelihood to rape, Malamuth reports that:

- About 10% of the population of male students is sexually aroused by "very extreme violence" with "a great deal of blood and gore" that "has very little of the sexual element" (Malamuth, 1985, p. 95).
- About 20% to 30% show substantial sexual arousal by depictions of rape in which the woman never shows signs of arousal, only abhorrence (p. 95).
- About 50% to 60% show some degree of sexual arousal by a rape depiction in which the victim is portrayed as becoming sexually aroused at the end (Malamuth, personal communication, August 18, 1986).

Given these findings, it is hardly surprising that after reviewing a whole series of related experiments, Neil Malamuth (1981b) concluded that "the overall pattern of the data is . . . consistent with contentions that many men have a proclivity to rape" (p. 139).

Unlike Malamuth's student-based studies, the men who completed Shere Hite's (1981) questionnaires about their self-reported desire to rape women came from all walks of life (p. 1123). Distinguishing between the men who revealed their identities and those who concealed them, Hite reports the following answers by the anonymous group to her question "Have you ever wanted to rape a woman?": 46% answered "yes" or "sometimes," 47% answered "no," and 7% said they had fantasies of rape (p. 1123). Presumably, the latter group had not acted them out—yet.

Surprisingly, the non-anonymous group of men reported slightly more interest in rape: 52% answered "yes" or "sometimes," 36% answered "no," and 11% reported having rape fantasies. (Could it be that many men don't think there is anything wrong with wanting to rape women?) Although Hite's survey was not based on a random sample, and therefore, like the experimental work cited above, cannot be generalized to the population at large, her finding that *roughly half of the more than 7,000 men she surveyed admitted to having wanted to rape a woman* on one or more occasions suggests that men's propensity to rape is probably very widespread indeed. It is interesting to note that the high percentages of men in Hite's study who admitted to wanting to rape a woman are comparable to the high percentage—44%—of women in my San Francisco probability sample of 930 women who reported having been the victim of one or more rapes or attempted rapes by men over the course of their lives (Russell, 1984).

The studies reviewed here suggest that at this time in U.S. history, a substantial percentage of the male population has some desire or proclivity to rape females. Indeed, some males in this culture consider themselves deviant for not wanting to rape a woman. Here is the statement of one of Hite's (1981) male respondents, for example:

> I have never raped a woman, or wanted to. In this I guess *I am somewhat odd.* Many of my friends talk about rape a lot and fantasize about it. The whole idea leaves me cold. (p. 719; emphasis added)

Another of Hite's male respondents made the following statement:

> I must admit a certain part of me would receive some sort of thrill at ripping the clothes from a woman and ravishing her. But I would probably collapse into tears of pity and weep with my victim, *unlike the traditional man.* (p. 719; emphasis added)

Some feminists are among the optimists who believe that males' proclivity to rape is largely a consequence of social and cultural forces, not biological ones. And, of course, having a *desire* to behave in a certain way is not the same as actually *behaving* in that way, particularly in the case of antisocial behavior. Nevertheless, it is helpful to have this kind of baseline information on the desires and predispositions of males, who are, after all, the chief consumers of pornography.

## PORNOGRAPHY AS A CAUSE OF RAPE: THEORY AND RESEARCH

As previously mentioned, smoking is not the only cause of lung cancer; nor is pornography the only cause of rape. I believe there are many factors that play a causal role in this crime.[4] I will not attempt to evaluate the relative importance of different causal factors in this book, but merely to show the overwhelming evidence that pornography is a major one of them.

Because all viewers of pornography are not equally affected by it, many people conclude that pornography cannot be playing a causative role in rape and other forms of violence against women. This is similar to the tobacco industry's defense of cigarette smoking. They maintain that because many smokers do not die of lung cancer, and because some nonsmokers *do* die of this disease, it is incorrect to believe that smoking causes lung cancer. But the tobacco industry's reasoning here is faulty. They have no grounds for assuming that the proponents of smoking as a cause of lung cancer believe that smoking is the *only* cause. In addition, the tobacco industry focuses on explaining individual rather than group differences, whereas the proponents of smoking as a cause of cancer focus on the higher number of lung cancer cases found in smokers as a group compared with nonsmokers as a group.

Similarly, instead of trying to explain why Mr. X is affected by viewing violent pornography while Mr. Y is not, it is necessary to look at whether the average aggression scores (or whatever is being measured) of those exposed to violent pornography are significantly higher than the aggression scores of those exposed to erotica or to nonsexual, nonaggressive material.

Whereas the individual level of analysis is more relevant for clinicians, the group level of analysis is more relevant to the makers of social policy. Had legislators insisted on being able to understand why Mr. A kept having car accidents when he drove while drunk but Mr. B did not before they imposed stiffer penalties on drunken drivers, there would have been even more deaths on the road. Although it can be important for researchers to try to explain individual differences, this information is not needed to determine the impact of pornography, or smoking, or drunk driving on large numbers or categories of people.

Sociologist David Finkelhor has developed a very useful multicausal theory to explain the occurrence of child sexual abuse. According to Finkelhor's (1984) model, in order for child sexual abuse to occur, four conditions have to be met. First, someone has to *want* to abuse a child sexually. Second, this person's internal inhibitions against acting out this desire have to be undermined. Third, this person's social inhibitions against acting out this desire (e.g., fear of being caught and punished) have to be undermined. Fourth, the would-be perpetrator has to undermine or overcome his or her chosen victim's capacity to avoid or resist the sexual abuse.

According to my theory, these four conditions also have to be met in order for rape, battery, and other forms of sexual assault on adult women to occur (Russell, 1984). Although my theory can be applied to other forms of sexual abuse and violence against women besides rape, this formulation of it will focus on rape because most of the research relevant to my theory has been limited to this form of sexual assault.

In *Sexual Exploitation* (1984), I suggest many factors that may predispose a large number of males in the United States to want to rape or assault women sexually. Some examples discussed in that book are (a) biological factors, (b) childhood experiences of sexual abuse, (c) male sex-role socialization, (d) exposure to mass media that encourage rape, and (e) exposure to pornography. Here I will discuss only the role of pornography.

Although women have been known to rape both males and females, males are by far the predominant perpetrators of sexual assault as well as the biggest consumers of pornography. Hence, my theory will focus on male perpetrators.

The major objective of this volume is to challenge the belief that pornography is harmless. However, this section focuses on rape because the research literature almost always separates rape from other forms of sexual violence. Furthermore, doing a comprehensive analysis of one form of sexual violence is sufficient to challenge the erroneous claim that pornography is harmless.

Despite my focus in this section on pornography as a cause of rape, this is only one type of harm that pornography promotes. I believe it is generally preferable to be aware of the commonality and frequently overlapping nature of the different manifestations of male violence. Beatings frequently accompany rape. Some rape victims are murdered. Sexual harassment sometimes involves rape. And the torture of women frequently has a sexual dimension. Hence, the pornographic pictures described in Part 2 included many different forms of violence against women, as well as misogynist material that was not violent.

A diagrammatic presentation of this theory appears in Figure 3.1. As previously noted, in order for rape to occur, a man must not only be predisposed to rape, but his internal and social inhibitions against acting out his rape desires must be undermined. My theory, in a nutshell, is that pornography (a) predisposes some males to want to rape women and intensifies the predisposition in other males already so predisposed; (b) undermines some males' internal inhibitions against acting out their desire to rape; and (c) undermines some males' social inhibitions against acting out their desire to rape.

## *The Meaning of "Cause"*

Given the intense debate about whether or not pornography plays a causal role in rape, it is surprising that so few of those engaged in it ever state what they mean by "cause." A definition of the concept of *simple causation* follows:

> An event (or events) that precedes and results in the occurrence of another event. Whenever the first event (the cause) occurs, the second event (the effect) necessarily or inevitably follows. Moreover, in simple causation the second event does

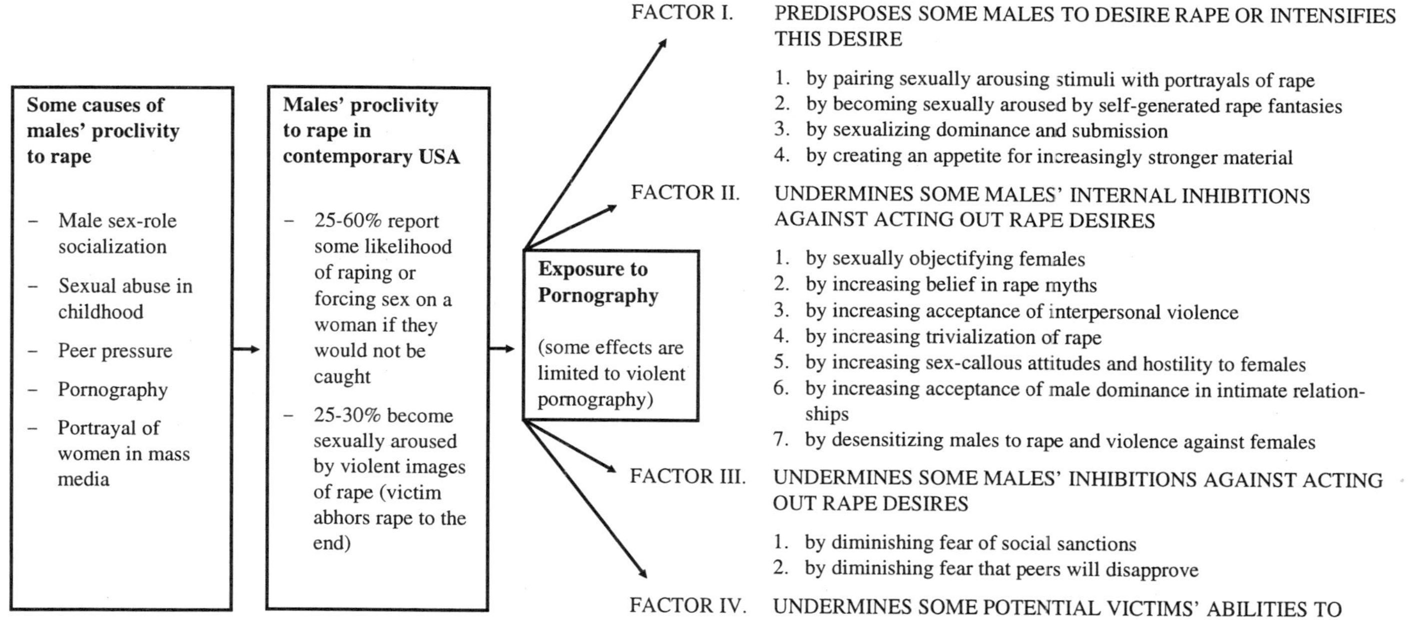


**Figure 3.1.** Theoretical Model of Pornography as a Cause of Rape

> not occur unless the first event has occurred. Thus the cause is both the SUFFICIENT CONDITION and the NECESSARY CONDITION for the occurrence of the effect. (Theodorson & Theodorson, 1979, p. 40)

By this definition, pornography clearly does not cause rape, as it seems safe to assume that some pornography consumers do not rape women and that many rapes are unrelated to pornography. However, the concept of *multiple causation* (defined below) *is* applicable to the relationship between pornography and rape.

> With the conception of MULTIPLE CAUSATION, various possible causes may be seen for a given event, any one of which may be a sufficient but not necessary condition for the occurrence of the effect, or a necessary but not sufficient condition. In the case of multiple causation, then, the given effect may occur in the absence of all but one of the possible sufficient but not necessary causes; and, conversely, the given effect would not follow the occurrence of some but not all of the various necessary but not sufficient causes. (Theodorson & Theodorson, 1979, p. 40)

As I have already presented the research on males' proclivity to rape, I will next discuss some of the evidence that pornography can be a sufficient (though not a *necessary*) condition for males to desire to rape (see the list on the far right of Figure 3.1). I will mention when the research findings I describe apply to violent pornography and when to pornography that appears to the viewer to be nonviolent.

## I. THE ROLE OF PORNOGRAPHY IN PREDISPOSING SOME MALES TO WANT TO RAPE

> I went to a porno bookstore, put a quarter in a slot, and saw this porn movie. It was just a guy coming up from behind a girl and attacking her and raping her. That's when I started having rape fantasies. When I seen [*sic*] that movie, it was like somebody lit a fuse from my childhood on up. . . . I just went for it, went out and raped. (Rapist interviewed by Beneke, 1982, pp. 73-74)

According to Factor I in my theoretical model, pornography can induce a desire to rape women in males who previously had no such desire, and it can increase or intensify the desire to rape in males who already have felt this desire. This section will provide the evidence for the four different ways in which pornography can induce this predisposition (they are listed in Factor I in Figure 3.1).

*1. Predisposes by Pairing of Sexually Arousing Stimuli With Portrayals of Rape.* The laws of social learning (e.g., classical conditioning, instrumental conditioning, and social modeling), about which there is now considerable consensus among psychologists, apply to all the mass media, including pornography. As Donnerstein (1983) testified at the hearings in Minneapolis: "If you assume that your child can learn from Sesame Street how to count one, two, three, four, five, believe me, they can learn how to pick up a gun" (p. 11). Presumably, males can learn equally well how to rape, beat, sexually abuse, and degrade females.

A simple application of the laws of social learning suggests that viewers of pornography can develop arousal responses to depictions of rape, murder, child sexual abuse, or other assaultive behavior. Researcher S. Rachman of the Institute of Psychiatry, Maudsley Hospital, London, has demonstrated that male subjects can learn to become sexually aroused by seeing a picture of a woman's boot after repeatedly seeing women's boots in association with sexually arousing slides of nude females (Rachman & Hodgson, 1968). The laws of learning that operated in the acquisition of the boot fetish can also teach males who were not previously aroused by depictions of rape to become so. All it may take is the repeated association of rape with arousing portrayals of female nudity (or clothed females in provocative poses).

Even for males who are not sexually excited during movie portrayals of rape, masturbation following the movie reinforces the association between rape and sexual gratification. This constitutes what R. J. McGuire, J. M. Carlisle, and B. G. Young refer to as "masturbatory conditioning" (Cline, 1974, p. 210). The pleasurable experience of orgasm—an expected and planned-for activity in many pornography parlors—is an exceptionally potent reinforcer. The fact that pornography is widely used by males as ejaculation material is a major factor that differentiates it from other mass media, intensifying the lessons that male consumers learn from it.

*2. Predisposes by Generating Rape Fantasies.* Further evidence that exposure to pornography can create in males a predisposition to rape where none existed before is provided by an experiment conducted by Malamuth. Malamuth (1981a) classified 29 male students as sexually force-oriented or non-force-oriented on the basis of their responses to a questionnaire. These students were then randomly assigned to view either a rape version of a slide-audio presentation or a mutually consenting version. The account of rape and the pictures illustrating it were based on a story in a popular pornographic magazine, which Malamuth describes as follows:

> The man in this story finds an attractive woman on a deserted road. When he approaches her, she faints with fear. In the rape version, the man ties her up and forcibly undresses her. The accompanying narrative is as follows: "You take her into the car. Though this experience is new to you, there is a temptation too powerful to resist. When she awakens, you tell her she had better do exactly as you say or she'll be sorry. With terrified eyes she agrees. She is undressed and she is willing to succumb to whatever you want. You kiss her and she returns the kiss." Portrayal of the man and woman in sexual acts follows; intercourse is implied rather than explicit. (p. 38)

In the mutually consenting version of the story the victim was not tied up or threatened. Instead, on her awakening in the car, the man told her that she was safe and "that no one will do her any harm. She seems to like you and you begin to kiss." The rest of the story is identical to the rape version (Malamuth, 1981a, p. 38).

All subjects were then exposed to the same audio description of a rape read by a female. This rape involved threats with a knife, beatings, and physical restraint. The victim was portrayed as pleading, crying, screaming, and fighting against the rapist (Abel, Barlow, Blanchard, & Guild, 1977, p. 898). Malamuth (1981a) reports that measures of penile tumescence as well as self-reported arousal "indicated that relatively high levels of sexual arousal were generated by all the experimental stimuli" (p. 33).

After the 29 male students had been exposed to the rape audio tape, they were asked to try to reach as high a level of sexual arousal as possible by fantasizing about whatever they wanted but without any direct stimulation of the penis (Malamuth, 1981a, p. 40). Self-reported sexual arousal during the fantasy period indicated that those students who had been exposed to the rape version of the first slide-audio presentation created more violent sexual fantasies than those exposed to the mutually consenting version *irrespective of whether they had been [previously] classified as force-oriented or non-force-oriented* (p. 33).

As the rape version of the slide-audio presentation is typical of what is seen in pornography, the results of this experiment suggest that similar pornographic depictions are likely to generate rape fantasies even in previously non-force-oriented male consumers. As Edna Einsiedel (1986) points out,

> Current evidence suggests a high correlation between deviant fantasies and deviant behaviors. . . . Some treatment methods are also predicated on the link between

> fantasies and behavior by attempting to alter fantasy patterns in order to change the deviant behaviors. (1986, p. 60)

Because so many people resist the idea that a desire to rape may develop as a result of viewing pornography, let us focus for a moment on behavior other than rape. There is abundant testimonial evidence that at least some males decide they would like to perform certain sex acts on women after seeing pornography portraying such sex acts. For example, one of the men who answered Shere Hite's (1981) question on pornography wrote: "It's great for me. *It gives me new ideas to try and see,* and it's always sexually exciting" (p. 780; emphasis added). Of course, there's nothing wrong with getting new ideas from pornography or anywhere else, nor with trying them out, as long as they are not actions that subordinate or violate others. Unfortunately, many of the behaviors modeled in pornography *do* subordinate and violate women, sometimes viciously.

The following statements about men imitating abusive sexual acts that they had seen in pornography were made by women testifying at the pornography hearings in Minneapolis, Minnesota, in 1983 (Russell, Part 1, 1993b). Ms. M testified that

> I agreed to act out in private a lot of the scenarios that my husband read to me. These depicted bondage and different sexual acts that I found very humiliating to do. . . . He read the pornography like a textbook, like a journal. When he finally convinced me to be bound, he read in the magazine how to tie the knots and bind me in a way that I couldn't escape. Most of the scenes where I had to dress up or go through different fantasies were the exact same scenes that he had read in the magazines.

Ms. O described a case in which a man

> brought pornographic magazines, books, and paraphernalia into the bedroom with him and told her that if she did not perform the sexual acts in the "dirty" books and magazines, he would beat her and kill her.

Ms. S testified about the experiences of a group of women prostitutes who, she said,

> were forced constantly to enact specific scenes that men had witnessed in pornography. . . . These men . . . would set up scenarios, usually with more than one woman, to copy scenes that they had seen portrayed in magazines and books.

For example, Ms. S quoted a woman in her group as saying,

> He held up a porn magazine with a picture of a beaten woman and said, "I want you to look like that. I want you to hurt." He then began beating me. When I did not cry fast enough, he lit a cigarette and held it right above my breast for a long time before he burned me.

Ms. S also described what three men did to a nude woman prostitute. They first tied her up while she was seated on a chair, then,

> They burned her with cigarettes and attached nipple clips to her breasts. They had many S and M magazines with them and showed her many pictures of women appearing to consent, enjoy, and encourage this abuse. She was held for twelve hours while she was continuously raped and beaten.

Ms. S also cited the following example of men imitating pornography:

> They [several johns] forced the women to act simultaneously with the movie. In the movie at this point, a group of men were urinating on a naked woman. All the men in the room were able to perform this task, so they all started urinating on the woman who was now naked.

When someone engages in a particularly unusual act previously encountered in pornography, it suggests that the decision to do so was inspired by the pornography. One woman, for example, testified to the *Attorney General's Commission on Pornography* (1986) about the pornography-related death of her son:

> My son, Troy Daniel Dunaway, was murdered on August 6, 1981, by the greed and avarice of the publishers of *Hustler* magazine. My son read the article "Orgasm of Death," set up the sexual experiment depicted therein, followed the explicit instructions of the article, and ended up dead. He would still be alive today were he not enticed and incited into this action by *Hustler* magazine's "How to Do" August 1981 article, an article which was found at his feet and which directly caused his death. (p. 797)

### *Children's Exposure to Pornography and Their Imitative Behavior*

Almost all the research on pornography to date has been conducted on men and women who were at least 18 years old. But as Malamuth (1985) points out, there is "a research basis for expecting that children would be more susceptible than adults to the influences of mass media, including violent pornography if they are exposed to it" (p. 107).

Psychologist Jennings Bryant (1985) testified to the Pornography Commission about a survey he had conducted involving 600 telephone interviews with males and females who were evenly divided into three age groups: students in junior high school, students in high school, and adults aged 19 to 39 years (p. 133). Bryant's interviews demonstrated that very large numbers of children now have access to both hard-core and soft-core materials. For example:

- The average age at which male respondents saw their first issue of *Playboy* or a similar magazine was 11 years (Bryant, 1985, p. 135).
- All the high school age males surveyed reported having read or looked at *Playboy, Playgirl,* or some other soft-core magazine (p. 134).
- High school males reported having seen an average of 16.1 issues of a soft-core magazine, and junior high school males said they had seen an average of 2.5 issues.
- In spite of being legally under age, junior high students reported having seen an average of 16.3 "unedited sexy R-rated films" (p. 135). (As previously pointed out, although R-rated movies are not usually considered pornographic, many of them meet my definition of pornography.)
- The average age of first exposure to sexually oriented R-rated films for all respondents was 12.5 years (p. 135).
- Nearly 70% of the junior high students surveyed reported that they had seen their first R-rated film before they were 13 years of age (p. 135).
- The vast majority of all the respondents reported exposure to hard-core, X-rated, sexually explicit material (p. 135). Eighty-four percent (84%) of the high school students had seen X-rated films, the average age of first exposure being 16 years, 11 months (p. 136). This is a higher percentage than was the case for any other age group, including adults.

When children imitate pornography, it is even more improbable than with adults that their behavior can be attributed entirely to their predispositions.

Bryant's (1985) respondents were asked if "exposure to X-rated materials had made them want to try anything they saw" (p. 140). Two thirds of the males reported "wanting to try some of the behavior depicted" (p. 140). Bryant reported that the desire to imitate what is seen in pornography "progressively increases as age of respondents *decreases*" (p. 140; emphasis added). Among the junior high school students, 72% of the males said that "they wanted to try some sexual experiment or sexual behavior that they had seen in their initial exposure to X-rated material" (p. 140).

In trying to ascertain if imitation had occurred, the respondents were asked: "Did you actually experiment with or try any of the behaviors depicted [within a few days of seeing the materials]?" (Bryant, 1985, p. 140). A quarter of the males answered that they had. A number of adult men answered "no," but said that some years later they had experimented with the behaviors portrayed. However, only imitations within a few days of seeing the materials were counted (p. 140). Male high school students were the most likely (31%) to report trying to enact the behaviors depicted (p. 141).

Unfortunately, no information is available on the behaviors imitated by these males. Imitating pornography is cause for concern only when the behavior imitated is violent or abusive, or when the behavior is not wanted by one or more of the participants. Despite this unfortunate oversight, Bryant's study is valuable in showing how common it is for males to *want* to imitate what they see in pornography, and for revealing that many *do* imitate it within a few days of viewing it. Furthermore, given the degrading and often violent content of pornography, as well as the youthfulness and susceptibility to influence of many of the viewers, how likely is it that these males imitated or wished to imitate only the nonsexist, nondegrading, and nonviolent sexual behavior depicted in the pornography?

James Check (1995) concurs with Malamuth that pornography "has a much greater effect on children than it does on adults. Fourteen-year-olds," he writes, "are exploring sexuality, desperate for information, and pornography provides what they think is useful information about sex" (p. 90). Unlike other researchers, Check has undertaken several surveys on children's exposure to adult pornography in Canada.

- In a survey of 1,100 children from 4 to 12 years old, Check (1995) found that 39% of them "said that they watched pornography at least once a month" (p. 89).
- Check replicated this study, administering it in shopping malls, theaters, and schools. "In each case," Check (1995) reported, "the results were the same: 39 percent" (p. 89).
- In another study conducted in Toronto by Check and Kristin Maxwell in 1992, 275 middle-class high school teenagers whose average age was 14 years were asked a number of questions on pornography. Check and Maxwell found that, "Nine out of ten boys (90 percent) and six out of ten girls (60 percent) had seen at least one pornographic movie. One-third of the boys, but only 2 percent of the girls, watched pornography at least once a month" (Check, 1995, p. 90; see also Check & Maxwell, 1992).

Of the 60% of girls who had seen at least one pornographic movie, Check (1995) reported that 58% had viewed only one "because a boyfriend or somebody wanted them to, or because they were curious, and then didn't want to watch again" (p. 90). Unlike the boys, very few of the girls were regular consumers.

The children were then given a list of six possible sources of sex education—teachers, peers, parents, books, schools, and magazines—and asked if pornography was an important source. Twenty-nine percent of the boys "said that pornography was *the most significant source* among those listed" (Check, 1995, p. 90; emphasis in the original). Check concluded that for the children he had studied, "some of them as young as six, seven, eight, nine, or ten years old—pornography *is* their sex education" (p. 91; emphasis in original).

With regard to what children learn from the pornography they see, Check and Maxwell (1992) reported that

> Many young boys indicated that they learned from pornography to connect the use of force during sex with excitement, with feeling stimulated. They also learned that force was justified if the female was at all active, i.e., if she took the initiative. . . . Forty-three percent of the boys and 16 percent of the girls said holding a girl down and forcing her to have intercourse if a boy has been sexually excited is at least "maybe okay" or said "I'm not sure." (p. 90)

Check (1995) also noted that it was the boys who said it was okay to hold a girl down and force her to have intercourse who were "overwhelmingly . . . the male teenagers who are reading and watching pornography" (p. 91).

Clearly, more research is needed on the effects of pornography on young male viewers, particularly in view of the fact that recent studies suggest that "over 50% of various categories of paraphiliacs [sex offenders] had developed their deviant arousal patterns prior to age 18" (Einsiedel, 1986, p. 53). Einsiedel also recommends that the age-of-first-exposure to pornography and the nature of that exposure should be examined more carefully because there is evidence that "the longer the duration of the paraphilia, the more significant the association with use of pornography" (p. 53).

*3. Predisposes by Sexualizing Dominance and Submission.* The first two ways in which pornography can predispose some males to desire rape, or intensify this desire (listed under Factor I in my theoretical model), both relate to the viewing of *violent* pornography. However, both violent *and* nonviolent pornography sexualizes dominance and submission. Hence, nonviolent pornography can also predispose some males to want to rape women.

James Check and Ted Guloien's (1989) distinctions among sexually violent pornography, nonviolent dehumanizing pornography, and erotica, and the contents of the videotapes they constructed to exemplify these three types of sexual materials, were described earlier (see Part 1, p. 9). Check and Guloien conducted an experiment in which they exposed 436 male Toronto residents and college students to one of the three types of sexual material over three viewing sessions, or to no sexual material. Subjects in the no-exposure condition (the control group) participated in only one session in which they viewed and evaluated a videotape that was devoid of sexual material.

These researchers investigated the impact of exposure to pornography and erotica on many variables, including the subjects' self-reported likelihood of raping and their self-reported sexually aggressive behavior. The latter behavior ranged from having coerced "a woman to engage in sexual intercourse by 'threatening to end the relationship otherwise,' to actually holding a woman down and physically forcing her to have intercourse" (Check & Guloien, 1989, pp. 165-166). Significantly, in an earlier study by Check and his colleagues, convicted rapists had scored three times higher on sexually aggressive behavior than had a control group of violent non-sex offenders (p. 166).

Following are some of the significant findings that Check and Guloien (1989) reported:

- "More than twice as many men who had been exposed to sexually violent or to nonviolent dehumanizing pornography reported that there was at least some likelihood that they would rape, compared to the men in the no-exposure condition"[5] (p. 177).
- "High-frequency consumers who had been exposed to the nonviolent, dehumanizing pornography subsequently reported a greater likelihood of raping, [and] were more sexually callous . . . than high-frequency pornography consumers in the no-exposure condition" (p. 176).
- "Exposure to the nonviolent, erotica materials did not have any demonstrated antisocial impact" (p. 178).

I pointed out earlier that men's self-reported likelihood of raping is not the best measure of *desire* to rape because this variable combines desire with the self-reported probability of acting out that desire. Nevertheless, since rape is clearly an act of dominance that forces submission, as are other coerced sex acts, Check and Guloien's finding that exposure to pornography increases men's self-reported likelihood of rape does offer tentative support for my theoretical model's claim that pornography predisposes some males to desire rape or intensifies this desire by sexualizing dominance and submission. Furthermore, this effect is not confined to violent pornography. It also makes sense theoretically that the sexualizing of dominance and submission would include the eroticization of rape and/or other abusive sexual behavior for some males.

For example, Ms. S testified at the pornography hearings in Minneapolis that

> Men constantly witness the abuse of women in pornography and if they can't engage in that behavior with their wives, girlfriends, or children, they force a whore to do it. (Russell, 1993b, p. 60)

And the Reverend Susan Wilhem testified in support of an anti-pornography ordinance in New York City that,

> I came across a picture [in pornography] of a position my ex-husband had insisted we try. When we did, I hemorrhaged for three days. My bruised cervix is still a problem after ten years. . . . We should have some place to go to complain about how pornography is part of making our husbands into rapists. (Russell, 1993b, p. 46)

Further research is needed to test the hypothesis that pornographic materials that sexualize dominance and submission would also serve to sexualize rape and other abusive sex acts. In addition, more researchers must follow the lead of Check and Guloien in differentiating between nonviolent degrading pornography and erotica.

*4. Predisposes by Creating an Appetite for Increasingly Stronger Material.* Dolf Zillmann and Jennings Bryant (1984) have studied the effects of what they refer to as "massive exposure" to pornography. (In fact, it was not particularly massive: 4 hours and 48 minutes per week over a period of 6 weeks. In later publications, Zillmann and Bryant use the term "prolonged exposure" instead of "massive" exposure.) These researchers, unlike Malamuth and Donnerstein, are interested in ascertaining the effects of nonviolent pornography and, in the study to be described, their sample was drawn from an adult nonstudent population.

Male subjects in the so-called *massive exposure* condition saw 36 nonviolent pornographic films, six per session per week; male subjects in the *intermediate* condition saw 18 such movies, three per session per week. Male subjects in the control group saw 36 nonpornographic movies. Various measures were taken after 1 week, 2 weeks, and 3 weeks of exposure. Information was also obtained about the kind of materials that the subjects were most interested in viewing.

Zillmann and Bryant (1984) report that as a result of massive exposure to pornography, "consumers graduate from common to less common forms" (p. 127), including pornography portraying "some degree of pseudoviolence or violence" (p. 154). These researchers suggest that this change may be "because familiar material becomes unexciting as a result of habituation" (p. 127).

According to Zillmann and Bryant's research, then, pornography can transform a male who was not previously interested in the more abusive types of pornography into one who *is* turned on by such material. This is consistent with Malamuth's findings (described on pp. 123-124) that males who did not previously find rape sexually arousing generate such fantasies after being exposed to a typical example of violent pornography.

## II. THE ROLE OF PORNOGRAPHY IN UNDERMINING SOME MALES' *INTERNAL* INHIBITIONS AGAINST ACTING OUT THEIR DESIRE TO RAPE

> The movie was just like a big picture stand with words on it saying "go out and do it, everybody's doin' it, even the movies." (Rapist interviewed by Beneke, 1982, p. 74)

Evidence has already been cited showing that 25% to 30% of males admit that there is some likelihood that they would rape a woman if they could be assured that they would get away with it. It is reasonable to assume that a substantially higher percentage of males would *like* to rape a woman but would refrain from doing so because of their internal inhibitions against these coercive acts. Presumably, the strength of these males' motivation to rape as well as their internal inhibitions against raping range from very weak to very strong, and also fluctuate in the same individual over time.

Seven ways in which pornography can undermine some males' internal inhibitions against acting out rape desires are listed in Figure 3.1. Research evidence substantiating each of these processes will be presented in the order in which they appear in this diagram.

*1. Objectifying Women.* Feminists have been emphasizing the role of objectification (treating females as sex objects) in the occurrence of rape for many years (e.g., Medea & Thompson, 1974; Russell, 1975). Males' tendency to objectify females makes it easier for them to rape girls and women. Check and Guloien (1989) note that other psychologists (e.g., Philip Zimbardo, H. C. Kelman) have observed that "dehumanization of victims is an important disinhibitor of cruelty toward others" (p. 161). The rapists quoted in the following passages demonstrate the link between objectification and rape behavior.

> It was difficult for me to admit that I was dealing with a human being when I was talking to a woman, because, if you read men's magazines, you hear about your stereo, your car, your chick. (Russell, 1975, pp. 249-250)

After this rapist had hit his victim several times in her face, she stopped resisting and begged him not to hurt her.

> When she said that, all of a sudden it came into my head, "My God, this is a human being!" I came to my senses and saw that I was hurting this person. (p. 249)

Another rapist said of his victim, "I wanted this beautiful fine *thing* and I got it" (Russell, 1975, p. 245; emphasis added).

Dehumanizing oppressed groups or enemy nations in times of war is an important mechanism for facilitating brutal behavior toward members of those groups. Ms. U, for example, testified that

> A society that sells books, movies, and video games like "Custer's Last Stand [Revenge]" on its street corners, gives white men permission to do what they did to me. Like they [her rapists] said, I'm scum. It is a game to track me down, rape and torture me. (Russell, 1993b)

The dehumanization of women that occurs in pornography is often not recognized because of its sexual guise and its pervasiveness. It is also important to note that the objectification of women is as common in nonviolent pornography as it is in violent pornography.

Doug McKenzie-Mohr and Mark Zanna (1990) conducted an experiment to test whether certain types of males would be more likely to objectify a woman sexually after viewing 15 minutes of nonviolent pornography. They selected 60 male students whom they classified into one of two categories: masculine sex-typed or gender schematic individuals who "encode all cross-sex interactions in sexual terms and all members of the opposite sex in terms of sexual attractiveness" (Bem, 1991, p. 361); and androgynous or gender aschematic males who do not encode cross-sex interactions and women in these ways (McKenzie-Mohr & Zanna, 1990, pp. 297, 299).

McKenzie-Mohr and Zanna (1990) found that after exposure to nonviolent pornography, the masculine sex-typed males "treated our female experimenter who was interacting with them in a professional setting, in a manner that was both cognitively and behaviorally sexist" (p. 305). In comparison with the androgynous males, for example, the masculine sex-typed males positioned themselves closer to the female experimenter and had "greater recall for information about her physical appearance" and less about the survey she was conducting (p. 305). The experimenter also rated these males as more sexually motivated based on her answers to questions such as, "How much did you feel he was looking at your body?" "How sexually motivated did you find the subject?" (p. 301).

This experiment confirmed McKenzie-Mohr and Zanna's hypothesis that exposure to nonviolent pornography causes masculine sex-typed males, in contrast to androgynous males, to view and treat a woman as a sex object.

2. *Rape Myths.* If males believe that women enjoy rape and find it sexually exciting, this belief is likely to undermine the inhibitions of some of those who would like to rape women. Sociologists Diana Scully (1985) and Martha Burt (1980) have reported that rapists are particularly apt to believe rape myths. Scully, for example, found that 65% of the rapists in her study believed that "women cause their own rape by the way they act and the clothes they wear"; and 69% agreed that "most men accused of rape are really innocent." However, as Scully points out, it is not possible to know if their beliefs preceded their behavior or constitute an attempt to rationalize it. Hence, findings from the experimental data are more telling for our purposes than these interviews with rapists.

Since the myth that women enjoy rape is widely held, the argument that consumers of pornography realize that such portrayals are false is totally unconvincing (Brownmiller, 1975; Burt, 1980; Russell, 1975). Indeed, several studies have shown that portrayals of women enjoying rape and other kinds of sexual violence can lead to increased acceptance of rape myths in both males and females. In an experiment conducted by Neil Malamuth and James Check (1985), for example, one group of college students saw a pornographic depiction in which a woman was portrayed as sexually aroused by sexual violence, and a second group was exposed to control materials. Subsequently, all subjects were shown a second rape portrayal. The students who had been exposed to the pornographic depiction of rape were significantly more likely than the students in the control group:

1. to perceive the second rape victim as suffering less trauma;
2. to believe that she actually enjoyed being raped; and

3. to believe that women in general enjoy rape and forced sexual acts. (Check & Malamuth, 1985, p. 419)

Other examples of the rape myths that male subjects in these studies are more apt to believe after viewing pornography are as follows:

- A woman who goes to the home or the apartment of a man on their first date implies that she is willing to have sex;
- Any healthy woman can successfully resist a rapist if she really wants to;
- Many women have an unconscious wish to be raped, and may then unconsciously set up a situation in which they are likely to be attacked;
- If a girl engages in necking or petting and she lets things get out of hand, it is her own fault if her partner forces sex on her. (Briere, Malamuth, & Check, 1985, p. 400)

In Maxwell and Check's 1992 study of 247 high school students (described above), they found very high rates of what they called "rape supportive beliefs," that is, acceptance of rape myths and violence against women. The boys who were the most frequent consumers of pornography, who reported learning a lot from it, or both, were more accepting of rape supportive beliefs than their peers who were less frequent consumers of pornography and/or who said they had not learned as much from it.

A quarter of girls and 57% of boys expressed the belief that it was at least "maybe okay" for a boy to hold a girl down and force her to have intercourse in one or more of the situations described by the researchers. In addition, only 21% of the boys and 57% of the girls believed that forced intercourse was "definitely not okay" in any of the situations. The situation in which forced intercourse was most accepted was when the girl had sexually excited her date. In this case, 43% of the boys and 16% of the girls stated that it was at least "maybe okay" for the boy to force intercourse on her (Maxwell & Check, 1992).

According to Donnerstein (1983), "After only 10 minutes of exposure to aggressive pornography, particularly material in which women are shown being aggressed against, you find male subjects are much more willing to accept these particular [rape] myths" (p. 6). These males are also more inclined to believe that 25% of the women they know would enjoy being raped (p. 6).

*3. Acceptance of Interpersonal Violence.* Males' internal inhibitions against acting out their desire to rape can also be undermined if they consider male violence against women to be acceptable behavior. Studies have shown that when male subjects view portrayals of sexual violence that have positive consequences—as they often do in pornography—it increases their acceptance of violence against women. Examples of some of the beliefs used to measure acceptance of interpersonal violence include the following:

- Being roughed up is sexually stimulating to many women;
- Sometimes the only way a man can get a cold woman turned on is to use force;
- Many times a woman will pretend she doesn't want to have intercourse because she doesn't want to seem loose, but she's really hoping the man will force her. (Briere et al., 1985, p. 401)

Malamuth and Check (1981) conducted an experiment of particular interest because the movies shown were part of the regular campus film program. Students were randomly assigned to view either a feature-length film that portrayed violence against women as being justifiable and having positive consequences (*Swept Away* or *The Getaway*) or a film without sexual violence. Malamuth and Check found that exposure to the sexually violent movies increased the male subjects' acceptance of interpersonal violence against women, but not the female subjects' acceptance of this variable. These effects were measured several days after the films had been seen.

Malamuth (1986) suggests several processes by which sexual violence in the media "might lead to attitudes that are more accepting of violence against women" (p. 4). Some of these processes also probably facilitate the undermining of pornography consumers' internal inhibitions against acting out rape desires.

1. Labeling sexual violence more as a sexual rather than a violent act.
2. Adding to perceptions that sexual aggression is normative and culturally acceptable.
3. Changing attributions of responsibility to place more blame on the victim.
4. Elevating the positive value of sexual aggression by associating it with sexual pleasure and a sense of conquest.
5. Reducing negative emotional reactions to sexually aggressive acts. (Malamuth, 1986, p. 5)

*4. Trivializing Rape*. According to Donnerstein (1985), in most studies on the effects of pornography, "subjects have been exposed to only a few minutes of pornographic material" (p. 341). In contrast, Zillmann and Bryant (1984) examined the impact on male subjects of what they refer to as "massive exposure" to nonviolent pornography (4 hours and 48 minutes per week over a period of 6 weeks; for further details about the experimental design, see page 131). After 3 weeks the subjects were told that they were participating in an American Bar Association study that required them to evaluate a trial in which a man was prosecuted for the rape of a female hitchhiker. At the end of this mock trial, various measures were taken of the subjects' opinions about the trial and about rape in general. For example, they were asked to recommend the prison term they thought most fair.

Zillmann and Bryant (1984) found that the male subjects who had been exposed to the massive amounts of pornography considered rape a less serious crime than they had before they were exposed to it; they thought that prison sentences for rape should be shorter; and they perceived sexual aggression and abuse as causing less suffering for the victims, even in the case of an adult male having sexual intercourse with a 12-year-old girl (p. 132). The researchers concluded that "heavy exposure to common nonviolent pornography trivialized rape as a criminal offense" (p. 117).

The more trivialized rape is in the perceptions of males who would like to rape women or girls, the more likely they are to act out their desires. Since the research cited above shows that exposure to pornography increases males' trivialization of rape, it is reasonable to infer that this process contributes to undermining some male consumers' internal inhibitions against acting out their desires to rape.

5. *Sex Callousness Toward Females*. In the same experiment on massive exposure, Zillmann and Bryant (1984) found that "males' sex callousness toward women was significantly enhanced" by prolonged exposure to pornography (p. 117). These male subjects, for example, became increasingly accepting of statements such as, "A woman doesn't mean 'no' until she slaps you"; "A man should find them, fool them, fuck them, and forget them"; and "If they are old enough to bleed, they are old enough to butcher." However, judging by these statements, it is difficult to distinguish sex callousness from a general hostility toward women.

Check and Guloien (1989) divided their sample of 436 male subjects into high-frequency pornography consumers (once per month or more often) and low-frequency pornography consumers (less than once per month). They found that the high-frequency pornography consumers scored significantly higher than the low-frequency consumers on sex callousness toward women (pp. 175-176). In addition, after high-frequency consumers had been exposed to the nonviolent, dehumanizing pornography, they became significantly more sexually callous toward women than the high-frequency consumers in the control group who had not been exposed to any sexual materials. The low-frequency consumers, on the other hand, were unaffected by exposure to the nonviolent dehumanizing pornography (p. 176).

Rapists as a group score higher than nonrapists on sex callousness and hostility toward women. Since the research cited above shows that exposure to pornography increases males' sex calloused attitudes toward women, it is reasonable to infer that this process contributes to undermining some male consumers' internal inhibitions against acting out their desires to rape.

*6. Acceptance of Male Dominance in Intimate Relationships.* A marked increase in males' acceptance of male dominance in intimate relationships was yet another result of the massive exposure to pornography (Zillmann & Bryant, 1984, p. 121). The notion that women are, or ought to be, equal in intimate relationships was more likely to be abandoned by these male subjects (p. 122). Finally, their support of the women's liberation movement also declined sharply (p. 134).

These findings demonstrate that pornography increases the acceptability of sexism. As Van White (1984) points out, "by using pornography, by looking at other human beings as a lower form of life, they [the pornographers] are perpetuating the same kind of hatred that brings racism to society" (p. 186).

For example, Ms. O testified about the ex-husband of a woman friend and next-door neighbor: "When he looked at the magazines, he made hateful, obscene, violent remarks about women in general and about me. He told me that because I am female I am here to be used and abused by him, and that because he is a male he is the master and I am his slave" (Russell, 1993b, p. 51).

Rapists as a group reveal a higher acceptance of male dominance in intimate relationships than nonrapists. Since Zillmann and Bryant's research shows that exposure to pornography increases males' acceptance of male dominance in intimate relationships, it is reasonable to infer that this process contributes to undermining some male consumers' internal inhibitions against acting out their desires to rape.

*7. Desensitizing Males to Rape.* In an experiment specifically designed to study desensitization, Donnerstein and Linz showed 10 hours of R-rated or X-rated movies over a period of 5 days to male subjects (Donnerstein & Linz, 1985, p. 34A). Some students saw X-rated movies depicting sexual assault; others saw X-rated movies depicting only consenting sex; and a third group saw R-rated sexually violent movies—for example, *I Spit on Your Grave, Toolbox Murders,* and *Texas Chainsaw Massacre.* Donnerstein (1983) describes *Toolbox Murders* as follows:

> There is an erotic bathtub scene in which a woman massages herself. A beautiful song is played. Then a psychotic killer enters with a nail gun. The music stops. He chases the woman around the room, then shoots her through the stomach with the nail gun. She falls across a chair. The song comes back on as he puts the nail gun to her forehead and blows her brains out. (p. 10)

According to Donnerstein, many young males become sexually aroused by this movie (p. 10).

Donnerstein and Linz (1985) described the impact of the R-rated movies on their subjects as follows:

> Initially, after the first day of viewing, the men rated themselves as significantly above the norm for depression, anxiety, and annoyance on a mood adjective checklist. After each subsequent day of viewing, these scores dropped until, on the fourth day of viewing, the males' levels of anxiety, depression, and annoyance were indistinguishable from baseline norms. (p. 34F)

By the fifth day, the subjects rated the movies as less graphic and less gory and estimated fewer violent or offensive scenes than after the first day of viewing. They also rated the films as significantly less debasing and degrading to women, more humorous, and more enjoyable, and reported a greater willingness to see this type of film again (Donnerstein & Linz, 1985, p. 34F). Their sexual arousal to this material, however, did not decrease over this 5-day period (Donnerstein, 1983, p. 10).

On the last day, the subjects went to a law school, where they saw a documentary reenactment of a real rape trial. A control group of subjects who had never seen the films also participated in this part of the experiment. Subjects who had seen the R-rated movies: (a) rated the rape victim as significantly more worthless, (b) rated her injury as significantly less severe, and (c) assigned greater blame to her for being raped than did the subjects who had not seen the films. In contrast, these effects were not observed for the X-rated nonviolent films.[6] However, the results were much the same for the violent X-rated films, despite the fact that the R-rated material was "much more graphically violent" (Donnerstein, 1985, pp. 12-13).

Donnerstein and Linz (1985) point out that critics of media violence research believe "that only those who are *already* predisposed toward violence are influenced by exposure to media violence" (p. 34F). This view is contradicted by the fact that Donnerstein and Linz actually preselected their subjects to ensure that they were not psychotic, hostile, or anxious; that is, they were not predisposed toward violence prior to the research.

Donnerstein and Linz's research shows that exposure to woman-slashing films (soft-core snuff pornography) increases males' desensitization to extreme portrayals of violence against women. It seems reasonable to infer that desensitization contributes to undermining some male viewers' internal inhibitions against acting out their desires to rape.

In summary: I have presented only a small portion of the research evidence for seven different effects of pornography, all of which probably contribute to the undermining of some males' internal inhibitions against acting out their rape desires. This list is not intended to be comprehensive.

## III. THE ROLE OF PORNOGRAPHY IN UNDERMINING SOME MALES' SOCIAL INHIBITIONS AGAINST ACTING OUT THEIR DESIRE TO RAPE

> I have often thought about it [rape], fantasized about it. I might like it because of having a feeling of power over a woman. But I never actually wanted to through *fear of being caught and publicly ruined*." (Male respondent, quoted in Hite, 1981, p. 715; emphasis added)

A man may want to rape a woman *and* his internal inhibitions against rape may be undermined by his hostility to women or by his belief in the myths that women really enjoy being raped and/or that they deserve it, but he may still not act out his desire to rape because of his *social* inhibitions. Fear of being caught and convicted for the crime is the most obvious example of a social inhibition. Fear of catching AIDS is another.

Shere Hite (1981) asked her male respondents whether or not they had ever wanted to rape a woman. In addition to the answer by one of them quoted above, a second man's reply was as follows:

> I have never raped a woman, but have at times felt a desire to—for the struggle and final victory. I'm a person, though, who always thinks before he acts, and *the consequences wouldn't be worth it. Besides I don't want to be known as a pervert.* (p. 715; emphasis added)

This man clearly assumes that if he acted out his desire to rape a woman, he would be caught and become known as a pervert. Hence, his fear of ruining his image or his reputation stopped him from becoming a rapist. What the other consequences were that deterred him is not clear, but they presumably include the prospect of arrest and perhaps incarceration. Note that he doesn't seem to be bothered by sometimes feeling a desire to rape. Judging from his statement, then, it seems clear that he is constrained by social factors, not internal ones, such as concern about traumatizing a woman or being wracked with guilt. The male respondent quoted at the beginning of this section reveals very similar motivation, and lack of internal inhibitions.

*1. Diminishing Fear of Social Sanctions.* In one of their early experiments, Malamuth et al. (1980) reported that after reading an account of a violent stranger rape, 17% of their male student subjects admitted that there was some likelihood that they might behave in a similar fashion were they to find themselves in the same circumstances. However, 53% of the same male students said there was some likelihood that they might act just as the rapist in the story did *if they could be sure of getting away with it.* The 36-percentage-point difference in these percentages reveals the significant role that can be played by social inhibitions against acting out rape desires. According to my theoretical model, pornography can and sometimes does undermine some males' social inhibitions against acting out their desire to rape.

In his content analysis of 150 pornographic home videos, Palys (1986) investigated "whether aggressive perpetrators [in these videos] ever received any negative consequences for their aggressive activity" (p. 32). For example, were charges laid, or did the perpetrator feel personal trauma as a result of his behavior, or did he get punished in any way? The answer was no to all of these questions in 73% of the cases in which an answer was ascertainable.

Similarly, Don Smith (1976a) found that fewer than 3% of the rapists portrayed in the 428 pornographic books he analyzed were depicted as experiencing any negative consequences as a result of their behavior. Indeed, many of them were rewarded. The common portrayal in pornography of rape as easy to get away with presumably contributes to the undermining of some males' social inhibitions against acting out their rape desires.

2. *Diminishing Fear of Disapproval by Peers.* Fear of disapproval by one's peers is another social inhibition that may be undermined by pornography. Zillmann (1985), for example, found that "massive" exposure to nonviolent pornography caused subjects to overestimate the number of people who engage in uncommon sexual practices, such as anal intercourse, group sexual activities, sadomasochism, and bestiality (p. 118). Rape is portrayed as a common male practice in pornography. The males who participate in pornography (the word *actor* is too euphemistic) may serve as a kind of pseudo-peer group and/or as role models for male consumers.

In short, male consumers may get the impression from the pornography they see that an endless supply of handsome middle-class males appear to have no compunction about raping women. They also appear to get a great kick out of it, and they don't lose face with their peers. For males who would like to rape a woman, or who think they would enjoy doing this, such portrayals may diminish their fear of being disapproved of by other males if they were to emulate the behavior of the men in pornography.

In general, I hypothesize the following disinhibiting effects of viewing violent pornography, particularly in "massive" amounts: (a) Viewers' estimates of the percentage of other males who have raped women would probably increase; (b) viewers would be likely to consider rape a much easier crime to commit than they had previously believed; (c) viewers would be less likely to believe that rape victims would report their rapes to the police; (d) viewers would be more likely to expect that rapists would avoid arrest, prosecution, and conviction in those cases that are reported; (e) viewers would become less disapproving of rapists and less likely to expect disapproval from others if they decided to rape. Further research is needed to evaluate these hypotheses.

## IV. THE ROLE OF PORNOGRAPHY IN UNDERMINING POTENTIAL VICTIMS' ABILITIES TO AVOID OR RESIST RAPE

> He . . . told me it was not wrong because they were doing it in the magazines and that made it O.K. (*Attorney General's Commission,* 1986, p. 786)

Obviously, this fourth factor (the role of pornography in undermining potential victims' abilities to avoid or resist rape) is not necessary for rape to occur. Nevertheless, once the first three factors in my causal model have been met—a male not only wants to rape a woman but is willing to do so because his inhibitions, both internal and social, have been undermined—a would-be rapist may use pornography to try to undermine a woman's resistance. Pornography is more likely to be used for this purpose when males attack their intimates (as opposed to strangers).

*1. Placing Females in High Rape-Risk Situations.* Most adult rape victims are not shown pornography in the course of being raped, although the testimony of prostitutes reveals that this is quite a common experience for many who are raped (*Everywoman,* 1988; Russell, 1993b). But pornography is more often used to try to persuade a woman or child to engage in certain acts, to legitimize the acts, and to undermine the woman's or child's resistance, refusal, or disclosure of these acts. Donald Mosher, for example, reported in his 1971 study that 16% of the "sex calloused" male students had attempted to obtain intercourse by showing pornography to a woman or by taking her to a "sexy" movie. When this strategy succeeds in manipulating women into so-called sex play, it can make women very vulnerable to date rape.

In a more recent study conducted in Canada, Charlene Senn (1992) found that "the more pornography women were exposed to, the more likely they were to have been forced or coerced into sexual activity they did not want." In addition, a male was present in most of the cases in which women were exposed to pornography. This suggests that most women who consume pornography do so because a man wants them to (Senn, 1992). This is a particularly important finding because the media have made much of the alleged fact that increasing numbers of women are renting pornographic videos, presuming that they do so for their own gratification.

There are at least two possible explanations for the positive correlation between the quantity of pornography to which women are exposed and their experiences of forced or coerced sex. It could be that women who cooperate with males' requests to view pornography are more likely to be sexually assaulted because viewing pornography somehow undermines their ability to avoid being sexually assaulted. Or, perhaps women who can be coerced into viewing pornography can also more easily be coerced sexually than women who refuse to view it.

Ms. M describes how her husband's continual pornography-related abuse of her during their years together almost drove her to suicide:

> I could see how I was being seasoned by the use of pornography and I could see what would come next. I could see more violence and I could see more humiliation, and I knew at that point I was either going to die from it—I would kill myself—or I would leave. And I felt strong enough to leave. ("Testimony From Public Hearings," 1993, p. 54).

When women are shown such materials, they probably feel more obliged to engage in unwanted sex acts that they mistakenly believe are normal. The Reverend Susan Wilhem, for example, testified about her ex-husband that pornography "made him expect that I would want to do crazy things" (Wilhem, 1993, p. 46). Evidence for this hypothesis is provided by Zillmann and Bryant's (1984) previously mentioned findings that massive exposure to pornography distorts the viewers' perceptions of sexuality by producing the lasting impression that relatively uncommon sexual practices are more common than they actually are; for example, "intercourse with more than one partner at a time, sadomasochistic actions, and animal contacts" (pp. 132-133).

The following two statements by two other women reveal how their husbands used pornography for this purpose.

> Once we saw an X-rated film that showed anal intercourse. After that he insisted that I try anal intercourse. I agreed to do so, trying to be the available, willing creature that I thought I was supposed to be. I found the experience very painful, and I told him so. But he kept insisting that we try it again and again. (*Attorney General's Commission,* 1986, p. 778)

> He told me if I loved him I would do this. And that, as I could see from the things that he read me in the magazines initially, a lot of times women didn't like it, but if I tried it enough I would probably like it and I would learn to like it. (*Everywoman,* 1988, p. 68)

More systematic research is needed to establish how frequently males use pornography to try to undermine women's ability to avoid or resist rape and other sexual abuse, and how effective this strategy is.

*2. A Pornography Industry That Requires the Exploitation of Females.* Because the portrayal of rape is one of the favorite themes of pornography, a large and ever-changing supply of girls and women have to be found to provide it. Clearly, some women are voluntary participants in simulated acts of rape, but many of the rapes that are photographed are real (see, e.g., *Everywoman,* 1988; Russell, 1993b).

In summary: A significant amount of research supports my theory that pornography can, and does, cause rape. Nevertheless, much of the research undertaken to date does not adequately examine the four key variables in my theory. Malamuth's concept of males' self-reported likelihood to rape women, for example, merges the notion of a *desire* to rape with my notion that internal inhibitions against acting out this desire can be undermined. So if a man says that there is some likelihood that he would rape a woman if he could get away with it, he is saying both that he has the desire to rape a woman *and* that his internal inhibitions against doing so are at least somewhat undermined (the degree of undermining depends on whether he is very likely, somewhat likely, or only slightly likely to do it).

I hope that more research will be guided in the future by the theoretical distinctions required by the model of pornography as a cause of rape that has been presented in this book.

## FURTHER EMPIRICAL FINDINGS ON PORNOGRAPHY AS A CAUSE OF RAPE

### *Further Evidence of Harm*

The 25% to 30% of male students who admit that there is some likelihood that they would rape a woman if they could be assured of getting away with it increases to 57% after exposure to sexually violent images, particularly sexually violent images depicting women enjoying rape (Donnerstein, 1983, p. 7). This means that *as a result of one brief exposure to pornography, the number of males who are willing to consider rape as a plausible act for them to commit actually doubles.*

One such brief exposure to pornography also increases male subjects' acceptance of rape myths and interpersonal violence against women. Given the hypothesis that such increased acceptance would serve to lower viewers' inhibitions against acting out violent desires, one would expect pornography consumption to be related to rape rates. This is what the following ingenious study found.

Larry Baron and Murray Straus (1984) undertook a 50-state correlational analysis of reported rape rates and the circulation rates of eight pornographic magazines: *Chic, Club, Forum, Gallery, Genesis, Hustler, Oui,* and *Playboy*. A highly significant correlation (+.64) was found between reported rape rates and circulation rates. Baron and Straus attempted to ascertain what other factors might possibly explain this correlation. Their statistical analysis revealed that the proliferation of pornographic magazines and the level of urbanization explained more of the variance in rape rates than the other variables investigated (e.g., social disorganization, economic inequality, unemployment, sexual inequality).

In another important study, Mary Koss conducted a large national survey of more than 6,000 college students selected by a probability sample of institutions of higher education (Koss, Gidycz, & Wisniewski, 1987). She found that college males who reported behavior that meets common legal definitions of rape were significantly more likely than college males who denied such behavior to be frequent readers of at least one of the following magazines: *Playboy, Penthouse, Chic, Club, Forum, Gallery, Genesis, Oui,* or *Hustler* (Koss & Dinero, 1989).

Several other studies have assessed the correlation between the degree of males' exposure to pornography and attitudes supportive of violence against women. Malamuth (1986) reports that in three out of four studies, "higher levels of reported exposure to sexually explicit media correlated with higher levels of attitudes supportive of violence against women" (p. 8).

1. Malamuth and Check (1985) conducted a study in which they found a positive correlation between the amount of sexually explicit magazines a sample of college males read and their beliefs that women enjoy forced sex.

2. Similarly, Check (1985) found that the more often a diverse sample of Canadian males were exposed to pornography, the higher their acceptance of rape myths, violence against women, and general sexual callousness was.

3. Briere, Corne, Runtz, and Malamuth (1984) found similar correlations in another sample of college males.

In her study of male sexuality, Shere Hite (1981) found that 67% of the males who admitted that they had wanted to rape a woman reported reading pornographic magazines, compared to only 19% of those who said that they had never wanted to rape a woman (p. 1123). With regard to the frequency of exposure to pornography, Hite reported that only 11% of the 7,000 males she surveyed said that they had never looked at pornography, 36% said they viewed it regularly, 21% said they did so sometimes, 26% said they did so infrequently, and 6% said that they had looked at it in the past (p. 1123). While correlation does not prove causation, and it therefore cannot be concluded from these studies that it was the consumption of the pornography that was responsible for the males' higher acceptance of violence against women, the studies' findings are consistent with a theory that a causal connection exists.

If the rape rate were very low in the United States, or if it had declined over the past few decades, such findings would probably be cited to support the view that pornography does not play a causative role in rape. While drawing such a conclusion would not be warranted, it is nevertheless of interest to note that my probability sample survey in San Francisco shows that a dramatic increase in the rape rate has occurred in the United States over the past several decades, during which there has also been a great proliferation of pornography (Russell, 1984). Unlike the rapes studied by Baron and Straus (1984), 90% of the rapes and attempted rapes described in my survey were never reported to the police.

With regard to experimental work, Donnerstein (1984) points out that "one cannot, for obvious reasons, experimentally examine the relationship between pornography and actual sexual aggression" (p. 53). He has, however, conducted experiments that show that the level of aggression of male subjects toward females increases after they have been exposed to violent pornography in which a female rape victim was portrayed as becoming aroused by the end of the movie. (Aggression was measured by the intensity of electric shock subjects were willing to administer; Donnerstein, 1984.) Violent films that were nonpornographic (depicting, for example, a man hitting a woman) also increased male subjects' levels of aggression toward women, but not to the same extent as violent pornographic films. When Donnerstein used violent pornography in which the victim was portrayed as being distressed by the sexual assault throughout the movie, the levels of aggression of male subjects toward females became increased only when they had first been angered by a confederate of the experimenter before seeing the movie.

To explain why male subjects' aggression toward women increases the most after seeing pornography that depicts a female rape victim becoming sexually aroused by the assault, Malamuth (1984) suggested that "positive victim reactions . . . may act to justify aggression and to reduce general inhibitions against aggression" (p. 36). This interpretation is consistent with my causal model's emphasis on the important role pornographic depictions play in undermining males' inhibitions against acting out hostile behavior toward women.

Many psychologists reject the use of attitudes as a basis for predicting behavior. Similarly, some people question whether Malamuth's measure of males' self-reported likelihood to rape has any meaningful relationship with their rape behavior. Hence, Malamuth's experiment to test whether males' attitudes and sexual arousal to depictions of rape can predict nonsexual aggression in the laboratory is of particular interest. A week after measuring male subjects' attitudes and sexual arousal to rape, they were angered by a female confederate of the experimenter. When the subjects were given an opportunity to behave aggressively toward her by administering an unpleasant noise as punishment for errors she made in an alleged extrasensory perception experiment, males who had higher levels of sexual arousal to rape and who had attitudes that condoned aggression "were more aggressive against the woman and wanted to hurt her to a greater extent" (Malamuth, 1986, p. 16). On the basis of this experiment, as well as two others, Malamuth concluded that "attitudes condoning aggression against women related to objectively observable behavior—laboratory aggression against women" (p. 16).

Both Donnerstein and Malamuth emphasize that their findings on the relationship between pornography and aggression toward women relate to aggressive or violent, not to nonviolent, pornography. Donnerstein (1984), for example, maintains that "nonaggressive materials only affect aggression when inhibitions to aggress are quite low, or with long-term and massive exposure. With a single exposure and normal aggressing conditions, there is little evidence that nonviolent pornography has any negative effects" (pp. 78-79). In the real world, however, inhibitions on aggressive behavior are often very low, and long-term and massive exposure to nonviolent material is also quite common. Furthermore, there is a lot of evidence of harm from nonaggressive pornography, aside from its impact on aggressive behavior (e.g., see Note 6 for my earlier discussion of some of Zillmann's findings).

Finally, given how saturated U.S. culture is with pornographic images and how much exposure many of the male subjects being tested have already had, the task of trying to design experiments that can show effects on the basis of one more exposure is challenging indeed. When no measurable effects result, it would be wrong, because of this methodological problem, to interpret the experiment as proving that there are no effects in general. We should focus, therefore, on the effects that do show up, rather than being overly impressed by the effects that do not.

Some people are critical of the fact that most of the experimental research on pornography has been conducted on college students, who are not representative of males in the general population. Hence, the research of Richard Frost and John Stauffer (1987) comparing the responses to filmed violence of college students and residents of an inner-city housing project is of particular interest.

In 5 of the 10 violent films shown to these two groups, the violence was directed at females. Frost and Stauffer (1987) evaluated these males' sexual arousal to these films by applying both self-report and physiological measures. They found that "there was no single form of violence for which the responses of the college sample exceeded those of the inner city sample on either measure" (p. 36). Four of the five most physiologically arousing categories of violence were the same for both groups: a female killing another female; a male killing a female; rape/murder; and a female killing a male (p. 37). Interestingly, depictions of male/female assault were the least exciting of all 10 types of violence measured to all subjects (p. 39).

The greatest disparity between the two groups in both physiological and self-reported sexual arousal was to depictions of rape, which "caused the highest response by inner-city subjects but only the fifth highest by the college sample" (Frost & Stauffer, 1987, p. 38). Although it is not acceptable to infer action from arousal, nevertheless, males who are aroused by depictions of violence toward women are more likely to act violently toward them than males who are not aroused by such depictions.

Hence, Frost and Stauffer's study suggests that college students are less prone to sexual violence than some other groups of males. This will come as no surprise to many people, as inner-city environments are more violent than colleges or than the places in which most college students grew up. One reason this finding is significant is that most of the research in this area has been conducted on college males. It is important to realize that the high percentages of male college students who admit that they might rape women, for example, might well be even higher if samples were drawn from nonstudent populations.

The exposure of sex offenders to pornography is another area of research that is relevant to the causal connections between pornography and rape. It is well known that many sex offenders claim that viewing pornography affects their criminal behavior. Ted Bundy is perhaps the most notorious of these males. For example, in one study of 89 nonincarcerated sex offenders conducted by William Marshall, "slightly more than one-third of the child molesters and rapists reported at least occasionally being incited to commit an offense by exposure to forced or consenting pornography" (Einsiedel, 1986, p. 62). Exactly a third of the rapists who reported being incited by pornography to commit an offense said that they deliberately used pornography in their preparation for committing the rape. The comparable figure for child molesters was much higher—53% versus 33% (p. 62).

However, as these sex offenders appear to have used the pornography to arouse themselves after they had already decided to commit an offense, it could be argued that it was not the pornography that incited them. To what extent they actually required the pornography in order to commit their offenses, like some perpetrators require alcohol, we do not know. Even if these perpetrators were eliminated from the data analysis, however, that still leaves 66% of the rapists and 47% of the child molesters who claimed that they were at least sometimes incited by pornography to commit an offense.

Gene Abel, Mary Mittelman, and Judith Becker (1985) evaluated the use of pornography by 256 perpetrators of sexual offenses, all of whom were undergoing assessment and treatment. Like Marshall's sample, these males were outpatients, not incarcerated offenders. This is important, because there is evidence that the data provided by incarcerated and nonincarcerated offenders differ (Einsiedel, 1986, p. 47). Abel and his colleagues reported that 56% of the rapists and 42% of the child molesters implicated pornography in the commission of their offenses. Edna Einsiedel (1986), in her review of the social science research for the 1985 Attorney General's Commission of Pornography, concluded that these studies "are suggestive of the implication of pornography in the commission of sex crimes among *some* rapists and child molesters" (p. 63; emphasis in original).

In another study, Michael Goldstein and Harold Kant found that incarcerated rapists had been exposed to hard-core pornography at an earlier age than males presumed to be nonrapists. Specifically, 30% of the rapists in their sexual offender sample said that they had encountered hard-core pornographic photos in their preadolescence (i.e., before the age of 11; Goldstein & Kant, 1973, p. 55.) This 30% figure compares with only 2% of the control group subjects exposed to hard-core pornography as preadolescents. (The control group was obtained by a random household sample that was matched with the offender group for age, race, religion, and educational level; Goldstein & Kant, 1973, p. 50). Could it be that this early exposure of the offenders to hard-core pornography played a role in making them rapists? It is hoped future research will address this question.

Some people argue that because there is some unknown number of men who have consumed pornography but who have never raped a woman, the theory that porn can cause rape is thereby disproven. This is comparable to arguing that because some cigarette smokers don't die of lung disease, there cannot be a causal relationship between smoking and lung cancer. Only members of the tobacco industry and some seriously addicted smokers consider this a valid argument today.

## NOTES

1. This survivor of pornography-related incestuous abuse testified at the Minneapolis hearings on pornography (*Public Hearings,* 1983).

2. I use the term *males* rather than *men* because many rapists are juveniles.

3. In 1984, Malamuth reported that in several studies, an average of about 35% of male students indicated some likelihood of raping a woman (p. 22). This figure has decreased to 25%–30% since then, for reasons Malamuth does not know (personal communication, July 1986).

4. See Russell (1984) for a multicausal theory of rape.

5. However, only the viewing of nonviolent dehumanizing materials resulted in male subjects reporting a significantly greater likelihood of engaging in other coercive sex acts than the control group. This unexpected finding deserves further investigation.

6. Why Donnerstein finds no effects for nonviolent pornographic movies while Zillmann reports many significant effects is not known.

# PART IV

## CONCLUSION

## INTRODUCTION

I believe that the rich and varied data now available from testimonies and many different kinds of research constitute convincing support for my theory that pornography—both violent and nonviolent—causes rape. For example:

- Preselected normal healthy male students say they are more likely to rape a woman after just one exposure to violent pornography.
- A large body of experimental research shows that the viewing of violent pornography results in higher rates of aggression against women by male subjects.
- Substantial research shows that nonviolent but degrading pornography (i.e., all pornography as opposed to erotica):

  a. promotes sexist attitudes that in turn promote rape (see Brownmiller, 1975; Medea & Thompson, 1974; Russell, 1975);

  b. promotes beliefs in rape myths; sex calloused attitudes toward women; beliefs in interpersonal violence; decreased support for equality between the sexes; decreased support for the women's liberation movement;

  c. promotes males to report an increased likelihood that they would rape a woman if they could get away with it.
- The laws of imitative learning apply to pornography at least as much as to the mass media in general. A high percentage of male junior high school students, high school students, and adults in a nonlaboratory survey report imitating X-rated movies within a few days of exposure.
- Similarly, the other laws of social learning apply to pornography at least as much as to the mass media in general. Indeed, I—and others—have argued that sexual arousal and orgasm are likely to serve as unusually potent reinforcers of the messages conveyed in pornography.
- Ten percent of a probability sample of 930 women in San Francisco, 9% of a sample of 640 women in Toronto, and 24% of female subjects in an experiment on pornography in Calgary, Canada, reported having been upset by requests to enact pornography (Russell, 1993b; Senn, 1993; Senn & Radtke, 1986). In addition, Evelyn Sommers and James Check (1987) reported that 39% of a sample of 44 battered women living in shelters in Toronto disclosed having been upset by requests to enact pornography.
- Hundreds of women have testified in public or in writing about how they have been victimized by pornography (*Attorney General's Commission,* 1986; *Public Hearings,* 1983; Russell, 1993b).

- A high percentage of prostitutes report that they have experienced pornography-related sexual assault (*Everywoman,* 1988; Russell, 1993b; Silbert & Pines, 1984).
- A high percentage of incarcerated and nonincarcerated rapists, child molesters, and serial killers have said that they have been incited by pornography to commit sexual crimes.

With so much evidence supporting a causal link between pornography and harm, Donnerstein's statement that the relationship between pornography and violence against women is stronger than the relationship between smoking and lung cancer is no exaggeration (see opening epigraph in Part 3).

This book has focused on providing theory, as well as visual and scientific evidence, that pornography causes rape. My theoretical framework for explicating the relationship between pornography and rape can be adapted to apply to other forms of sexual assault and abuse, as well as to woman battering and femicide (the misogyny-motivated killing of women).

I have done the preliminary work on adapting it to demonstrate a causal connection between adult and child pornography and child sexual abuse. As with rape, I do not contend that pornography is the only cause of child sexual abuse, but that it is one of several causal factors. This theory, the research literature and first-person testimonies that support it, and a description and analysis of child pornography in mainstream pornographic magazines, will be included in a companion volume to *Dangerous Relationships*.

### *The Irrationality of Pro-Porn Feminists*

Of particular concern to anti-porn feminists is Zillmann's (1985) finding that after exposure to pornography, both male and female subjects become more antagonistic to the goals of the women's liberation movement, including gender equality (see Part 3, p. 138). It is shocking, contradictory, and extraordinarily foolish that so many women who support and even fight for the liberation of women also champion, tolerate, or don't care about pornography, despite the solid evidence that it undermines our goals.

The National Organization for Women (NOW), the largest and most enduring feminist organization in the world (a kind of NAACP of the women's movement) refuses to denounce pornography as harmful to women. Although NOW still has excellent anti-porn statements on record—statements that were formulated in earlier years when most feminists opposed pornography—the organization will no longer publicly endorse these statements. When I asked NOW president this otherwise suave and charming speaker fell apart, refused to answer my question, and became actively hostile (see Russell, 1996a).

On another occasion I attended a disturbing speaker panel at the University of California, Berkeley, where several leaders and spokeswomen from San Francisco NOW explained their pro-porn views to the audience. Included on the panel was NOW official Miki Demarest, who expressed great pride in the fact that she was the publisher of *The Spectator,* a pornographic rag sold in stores and street-corner vending machines in the East Bay region. Her paper contains articles on the joys of incest and sexual violence for both perpetrators and victims, and is available to anyone, including children, with a couple of quarters to spend.

Another NOW panelist talked about the gratification and power she obtained from being a prostitute despite the fact that it must be one of the most dangerous forms of employment in the world, to say nothing of the sexual exploitation intrinsic to it. (This panelist actually used the term *sex worker*—a term I avoid because I reject the view that the work of prostitutes is similar to other service jobs [see Note 2].) These women and their pro-porn, pro-prostitution views enjoy considerable support in NOW.

With regard to prostitution (I see pornography "actresses" as prostitutes[1]), many people would be dismayed to learn that a resolution was passed at NOW's annual conference in 1973 favoring the decriminalization of prostitution.[2] Although this policy was described as "an interim measure" when it was voted on, it remains NOW's policy on prostitution 24 years later. Also shocking is this feminist organization's description of the relationship between prostitutes and their pimps. NOW sees fit to characterize prostitutes as surrendering their earnings to pimps "in exchange for his economic and psychological support"! (NOW, 1973). In reality, pimps typically treat "their girls," "their bitches," or "their hos" as their personal possessions and beat them to a pulp if they think or behave otherwise. A power relationship in which prostitutes are subject to domination, violence, and torture by their pimps, as well as theft of their earnings, would be a more apt description.

## AMERICAN PUBLIC OPINION ON PORNOGRAPHY

As the public opinion poll data presented in this section will show, only a minority of Americans believe that pornography is harmless and that the current laws against it are adequate. Nevertheless, pornography is ubiquitous in this society and proliferates daily. (As discussed in Part 1, the circulation of porn magazines has been declining over the past decade, but this is primarily due to the burgeoning markets in video pornography, computer pornography, and pornography on the Internet.) This means that the minority of pro-pornography citizens are imposing their wishes on the majority. I will also argue that it is the minority in favor of pornography who are the censors of those who recognize that pornography is harmful, despite the former's vociferous claims to the contrary.[3]

### *Public Opinion on the Impact of Pornography*

*1. Pornography and Rape.* Public opinion polls from 1985 to 1994 show that the majority of U.S. citizens believe that pornography causes men to rape.

According to a Gallup poll conducted for *Newsweek* in 1985 (titled "Mixed Feelings on Pornography"), 73% of a national sample of 1,020 adults believed that "explicit sexual magazines, movies and books . . . *lead some people to commit rape or sexual violence*" (Press et al., 1985, p. 60; emphasis mine; see Table A.2.1 in Appendix 2). Eight years later, in 1993, the National Opinion Research Center reported that 57% of a national sample of 2,992 adults believed that "sexual materials *lead people to commit rape*" (emphasis mine; see Table A.2.3a in Appendix 2). And one year later, in 1994 (the "General Social Survey" of January 27, 1994), the same polling firm reported that this figure had dropped to 48% for the identical question (see Table A.2.3a in Appendix 2). Even though this last percentage is less than 50%, it is higher than the 42% who believe that sexual materials do *not* lead people to commit rape. It should also be noted that 62% of the *women* polled in 1993 and 55% of those polled in 1994 believed that sexual materials lead people to commit rape (see Appendix 2, Table A.2.3b).

What might explain this marked decline in the percentages of individuals, as well as of women, who believe that pornography causes some men to commit rape?[4]

First, this decline could reflect the success of the massive propaganda campaign organized in 1986 by the Media Coalition to discredit the 1985 Attorney General's Commission on Pornography's conclusion that pornography causes violent and criminal behavior and is harmful to women. This Coalition, which included the American Booksellers Association, the Association of American Publishers, the Council of Periodical Distributors, the International

Periodical Distributors Association, and the National Coalition of College Stores, hired a Washington, D.C.-based public relations firm to conduct this campaign.[5] I believe this campaign had a great impact on public opinion.

Second: Pornography has expanded into a multi-billion-dollar-a-year industry, and I believe we are seeing on a massive scale some of the effects so brilliantly and carefully documented by Malamuth, Donnerstein, Zillmann, and their colleagues (described in Part 3). For example, as already mentioned, Zillmann and Bryant (1984) discovered that one of the effects of viewing pornography, including nonviolent pornography, is that "the more extensive the exposure, the more accepting of pornography subjects became" (p. 133). Although females expressed significantly less acceptance of pornography than males, this effect also occurred with female subjects.

The more tolerant people are of pornography, the more it becomes part of mainstream culture; the more it becomes part of the mainstream culture, the more that previously critical people are subjected to it; the more that previously critical people are subjected to it, the more tolerant of it they become. Zillmann and Bryant's finding suggests a kind of cycle theory of ever-increasing tolerance by the American public toward pornography.

Third: Donnerstein's description of the desensitization that occurred in healthy preselected male students after only 5 days of viewing woman-slashing films may apply to ever-growing segments of our society (Donnerstein, Linz, & Penrod, 1987). Although Donnerstein stakes a great deal on differentiating woman-slashing films and pornography, I have argued above that these R-rated films clearly meet my definition of pornography.

Regardless of the validity of the three explanations suggested, if we extrapolate from the results of these three surveys to the general population, it is evident that the majority of U.S. citizens continue to believe that pornography harms women by causing rape. Aside from rape, there are many other ways in which the majority of Americans believe that pornography is harmful. For example:

2. *Respect for Women.* According to the Gallup poll survey in 1985 (titled "Mixed Feelings on Pornography"), 76% of the respondents believe that "explicit sexual magazines, movies and books . . . *lead some people to lose respect for women*" (emphasis mine; see Appendix 2, Table A.2.1).

3. *Impact on Public Morals.* According to the 1985 Gallup poll survey cited above, 67% of the respondents believe that "explicit sexual magazines, movies

and books . . . *lead to a breakdown of public morals*" (emphasis mine; see Appendix 2, Table A.2.1). In 1993, the National Opinion Research Center (the "General Social Survey" of February 5, 1993) reported that 64% of a national sample of 2,992 adults believed that "sexual materials *lead to a breakdown of morals*" (emphasis mine; see Table A.2.3a in Appendix 2). And one year later, in 1994 (the "General Social Survey" of January 27), the same polling firm reported that this figure had dropped to 57% for the identical question (see Table A.2.3a in Appendix 2). This 10% drop over almost a decade is significant but nevertheless much smaller than the 25% decline over the same period in respondents believing that pornography causes rape.

Once again, extrapolating from the results of these three surveys to the general population, it is evident that a significant majority of Americans believe that pornography causes a breakdown of morals. If this belief is correct, it is a seriously destructive effect of pornography.

*4. Nude Magazines and X-Rated Movies.* According to a poll conducted by Princeton Survey Research Associates in 1994 ("People, the Press & Politics: New Political Landscape"), 44% of a national sample of 1,009 adults agreed that "*nude magazines and X-rated movies provide harmless entertainment for those who enjoy it*" compared with 54% who disagreed with this statement (emphasis mine; see Appendix 2, Table A.2.4).

*5. The Impact of Pornography on Children.* According to a poll conducted by Voter/Consumer Research in 1993 (titled "National Family Values"), 64% of a national sample of 1,100 adults *strongly* agreed with the statement that "*children are harmed by the presence of sexually explicit materials and adult entertainment in our society,*" and 20% agreed "somewhat" with this statement (emphasis mine; see Appendix 2, Table A.2.2). Extrapolating from the results of this survey to the general population, we can infer that an astounding 84% of Americans believe that the mere existence of pornography in society harms children.

*6. Pornography on the Internet.* According to a poll conducted by Princeton Survey Research Associates in 1995, 67% of a national sample of 752 adults reported being "*very* concerned" about *pornography being too available to young people on the Internet,* and an additional 18% reported being "somewhat" concerned: that is, 85% expressed at least some concern (emphasis mine; see Appendix 2, Table A.2.5).

This section has reported the findings of a substantial number of public opinion polls conducted by different reputable polling firms, all of which confirm that the majority of U.S. inhabitants believe that pornography is harmful to women and to society in a multiplicity of ways. The next section shows that the majority of Americans want greater legal restrictions to be imposed on pornography in this country.

## *Public Opinion on Americans' Desire for Greater Legal Restrictions on Pornography*

*1. Laws to Ban Violent Pornography.* According to the public opinion poll conducted by Gallup on a national sample of 1,020 adults in 1985 (titled "Mixed Feelings on Pornography," cited above):

- 73% favored laws that would totally ban "magazines that show sexual violence"
- 68% favored laws that would totally ban "theaters showing movies that depict sexual violence"
- 63% favored laws that would totally ban the "sale or rental of video cassettes featuring sexual violence" (see Table A.2.7 in Appendix 2).
- Only 6%, 9%, and 13%, respectively, favored no restrictions on these different forms of pornography.

*2. Government Restrictions on Portrayals of Explicit Sex in the Media.* According to a public opinion poll conducted by Princeton Survey Research Associates on a national sample of 1,494 adults in 1994 (the "Eight Nation & The Press Survey"), 59% favored *government restrictions on portrayals of explicit sex in magazines and newspapers as well as on television and radio,* compared with 36% who opposed such restrictions (see Appendix 2, Table A.2.8).

*3. Need Stricter Laws to Control Pornography.* According to a public opinion poll conducted by Hart and Teeter Research Companies on a national sample of 1,502 adults in 1994, 55% strongly agreed with the statement that "*We need stricter laws to control pornography in books and movies*"; 22% agreed "somewhat"; and 21% disagreed strongly or somewhat (emphasis mine; see Table A.2.9 in Appendix 2). This means that well over three times more of the respondents favored stricter laws than were opposed to this idea. This constitutes a very large majority.

*4. Pornography on the Internet.* According to a public opinion poll conducted by Princeton Survey Research Associates on a national sample of 3,603 adults in 1995 ("Technology and On-Line Use Survey"), 52% favored "*a law that would make it illegal for a computer network to carry pornographic or adult material,*" compared with 41% who were opposed to such a law (emphasis mine; see Table A.2.10 in Appendix 2).

The public opinion polls cited above make it clear that a majority of American citizens, often a very large majority, believe that pornography appearing in a range of different formats is harmful to women, young people, children, and society at large.

A majority of citizens also favor stricter legal regulations against pornography in all forms of mass media. What, then, might explain why the minority of Americans who are pro-pornography are able to prevent the majority from having their wishes met? The next section will address this question.

## THE POWER OF PRO-PORN AMERICANS TO DOMINATE THE MAJORITY OF ANTI-PORN AMERICANS

Those who believe that pornography is harmless and that it should not be restricted, or that the current restrictions on it should not be increased, form a kind of power elite that imposes its views of pornography on the less powerful members of American society. They are disproportionally males with college or postgraduate education who are well-off financially—as the public opinion data to be cited will show. Many of them are also in occupations that enable them to suppress or censor views with which they disagree. They are disproportionally employed in publishing, educational institutions (particularly higher education), the arts, the mass media, the entertainment industry, and library services—professions whose members are disproportionally supportive of pornography. Because of their power to influence public opinion, and even to seem to represent it, they can make it appear that their minority view is actually a majority one.

### *Public Opinion Data*

*1. Gender of Respondents.* Only a few of the public opinion poll tables in Appendix 2 provide data on the relationship between certain demographic and ideological variables and opinions on pornography. In one of these studies conducted in 1993, 62% of the women respondents believed that pornography in the form of books, movies, magazines, and photographs "*lead people to commit rape,*" compared with 50% of men respondents (see Table A.2.3b in Appendix 2). One year later, in 1994, the respective figures were 55% for women and 40% for men (emphasis mine; see Table A.2.3b in Appendix 2). While these percentages differ by only 12 percentage points and 15 percentage points, respectively, they are likely to be statistically significant given the large sample sizes on which they are based (2,992 and 1,606, respectively).

In the same two studies, 69% of the women respondents believed that pornography *leads to a breakdown of morals* compared with 57% of men (1993). One year later, in 1994, the respective figures were 64% for women and 49% for men (see Table A.2.3b in Appendix 2).

In a third study, conducted in 1995, 77% of the women respondents reported being "*very* concerned" about *pornography being too available to young people on the Internet,* compared with 56% of the men respondents (a 21-percentage point difference; emphasis mine; see Appendix 2, Table A.2.6).

Moreover, in a fourth study, conducted in 1994, 68% of the women respondents strongly agreed with the statement, "*We need stricter laws to control pornography in books and movies,*" compared with only 41% of the men respondents (a 27-percentage point difference; emphasis mine; see Table A.2.9 in Appendix 2).

2. *Education of Respondents.* There tends to be a more or less linear relationship between the respondents' education and their opinions on pornography. In 1993, while 69% of the respondents who did not graduate from high school believed that *pornography leads people to commit rape,* only 44% of those who graduated from college subscribed to this belief (a 25-percentage point difference; see Table A.2.3b in Appendix 2). One year later, in 1994, the respective figures for education and believing that pornography leads people to commit rape were 61% for the respondents who did not graduate from high school and 37% for those who graduated from college (a 24-percentage point difference; see Table A.2.3b in Appendix 2). The only exception to these linear relationships is that respondents with postgraduate educations were not quite as pro-pornography as the college graduates.

Similarly, while 75% of the respondents who did not graduate from high school in 1993 believed that *pornography leads to a breakdown of morals,* only 47% of the respondents with postgraduate education shared this belief (a 28-percentage point difference; see Table A.2.3b in Appendix 2). One year later, in 1994, the respective figures for education and believing that pornography leads to a breakdown of morals were 64% for the respondents who did not graduate from high school and 47% for those who graduated from college (a 17-percentage point difference; see Table A.2.3b in Appendix 2). The only exception to a perfectly linear relationship here is that respondents with post-graduate educations were less inclined to believe that pornography leads to a breakdown in morals than the college graduates.

The relationship between the respondents' education and their strong agreement with the view that, "*We need stricter laws to control pornography in books and movies*" was also completely linear: Seventy-four percent of those who had not graduated from high school strongly agreed that stricter laws were needed compared with only 39% of those with a postgraduate education (a 35-percentage point difference; emphasis mine; see Table A.2.9 in Appendix 2).

*3. Income of Respondents.* As with education, the relationship between the respondents' income and their opinions on pornography was also more or less linear. For example, while 71% of the respondents with the lowest incomes (less than $15,000) believed that *pornography leads people to commit rape,* only 41% of the respondents with the highest incomes ($75,000 and over) believed that pornography leads people to commit rape (a 30-percentage point difference; see Table A.2.3b in Appendix 2). One year later, the comparable percentages ranged from 58% for the poorest group to 34% for the richest group (a 24-percentage point difference; see Table A.2.3b in Appendix 2).

While 72% of the respondents with incomes of less than $15,000 believed that *pornography leads to a breakdown in morals,* only 54% of the respondents with incomes of $75,000 and over subscribed to this belief (an 18-percentage point difference; see Table A.2.3b in Appendix 2). One year later, the comparable percentages ranged from 62% for the poorest group to 49% for the richest group (a 13-percentage point difference; see Table A.2.3b in Appendix 2).

The relationship between the respondents' incomes and their strongly agreeing with the view that "*We need stricter laws to control pornography in books and movies*" was almost completely linear: 72% of those with incomes of less than $15,000 strongly agreed that stricter laws were needed compared with only 40% of those with incomes of $75,000 and over (a 32-percentage point difference; see Table A.2.9 in Appendix 2).

*4. The Ethnicity of Respondents.* Because there is obviously a relationship between ethnicity, power, privilege, and influence, it seems reasonable to expect that this factor would also be associated with opinions on pornography. If this is the case, it is not consistently reflected in these opinion polls. For example, almost identical percentages of "Blacks" and "Whites" (the categories used in the poll) in both 1993 and 1994 believed that *pornography leads people to commit rape* (see Table A.2.3b in Appendix 2). And slightly more whites than blacks believed that *pornography leads to a breakdown of morals*—a 7-percentage point difference in 1993 and a 9-percentage point difference in 1994 (see Table A.2.3b in Appendix 2).

On the other hand, blacks expressed much greater concern than whites that *Internet pornography is too available to young people:* 91% of the black respondents were *very* concerned compared to only 64% of whites (a 27-percentage point difference; see Table A.2.6 in Appendix 2). Only 62% of Asians, who were separately identified in this poll, were very concerned, virtually the same percentage as for whites.

A higher percentage of black respondents than white also strongly agreed that *stricter laws to control pornography are needed:* 69% versus 52% (a 17-percentage point difference; see Table A.2.9 in Appendix 2). Although higher percentages of Asian and Hispanic than white respondents strongly agreed that stricter laws to control pornography were needed, the differences were much smaller than for blacks: 58% for Asians and 62% for Hispanics (differences of only 6-percentage points and 10-percentage points, respectively; see Table A.2.9 in Appendix 2).

With the exception of ethnicity, these public opinion polls support the thesis that it is the haves rather than the have-nots who are pro-pornography. It seems reasonable to infer that well-educated, affluent men have the power and influence to impose their views of pornography on those with much less power and influence—women, the less well-educated, and the less well-off—and, furthermore, that they use their power for this purpose.

Despite the many years that this elite sector of society has had to try to brainwash others into believing that pornography is a harmless fantasy that is cathartic for consumers, and that women in the industry have freely chosen this line of work and are not being exploited and destroyed physically and psychologically by doing it, the public opinion poll data make it clear that this elite has not yet succeeded in convincing the majority of Americans to accept this drivel. But accept it or not, the educated elite are the ones whose views on pornography have been implemented. So much for democracy.

I noted in Part 1 that anti-porn feminists are typically denounced as pro-censorship because we, too, believe that pornography promotes rape and other kinds of harm to women. However, the above analysis of public opinion poll data shows that it is the people who *defend* pornography, particularly men, who are the censors of those of us who recognize the destructive effects of pornography on women and society.

## CONCLUSION

Noting that violent crime among children between the ages of 13 and 17 increased 126% between 1976 and 1992, the American Medical Association (AMA) identified media violence as "partly responsible" ("Parents Find Violent TV a Turnoff," 1996, p. A2). The AMA has drawn up a Physicians Guide to Media Violence that "gives doctors suggestions on how to talk to parents about children's viewing habits and how to advise them about making changes" that will be distributed to 60,000 doctors "to help combat the effect television and movie violence has on children" ("Parents Find Violent TV a Turnoff," 1996, p. A2).

Unfortunately, but not surprisingly, the AMA does not include pornography in their assessment of the media as a causal factor in children's violent behavior. Given the widespread exposure of young males to pornography magazines and X-rated videos (documented in Part 3), there is no logical reason to exclude it. If watching violent and abusive material on TV and in mainstream movies causes violent behavior in children, it follows that children who view pornography will also be affected by it.

People often chide those of us who focus on criticizing misogyny in pornography with remarks like, "Why are you more concerned about the violence in pornography than the violence on television?" One of my answers to this question is that many feminists and nonfeminists protest the violence on television, but very few feminists are willing to protest, or even seriously look at, pornography. Therefore, those of us who are willing to confront pornography deserve congratulations rather than castigation.

Neil Malamuth (1989) provides another good answer to this question by noting the following very important differences between the portrayal of nonsexual violence in the mainstream mass media and sexual violence in pornography:

> Males act against females in the vast majority of sexually aggressive depictions . . . , whereas the victim is usually male in nonsexual portrayals of violence. (p. 167)

> Victims of nonsexual aggression are usually shown as outraged by their experience and intent on avoiding victimization. They, and at times the perpetrators of the aggression, suffer from the violence. However, when sexual violence is portrayed, there is frequently the suggestion that, despite initial resistance, the victim secretly desired the abusive treatment and eventually derived pleasure from it. This provides a built-in justification for aggression that would otherwise be considered unjustifiable. Sexual violence is often presented as without negative consequences for either the victim of the perpetrator. (p. 167)

Unlike nonsexual violence, pornography is designed to arouse males sexually:

> Such arousal in response to sexually violent depictions might result in subliminal conditioning and cognitive changes in the consumer by associating physical pleasure with violence. Therefore, even sexual aggression depicted negatively may have harmful effects because of the sexual arousal induced by the explicitness of the depiction. For example, a person who views a sexually violent scene might feel that the violence is immoral but may nonetheless be sexually aroused by it. Such arousal might motivate him to rationalize the aggression or to minimize its seriousness or its consequences. (Malamuth, 1989, p. 167)

In contrast to all those who fail to recognize the devastating effects of the pornography that permeates our society, Van White (1984), an African American man who chaired the Hearings on Pornography in Minneapolis in 1983, commented as follows on the impact of the testimony by the survivors of pornography-related abuse:

> These horror stories made me think of the history of slavery in this country—how Black women were at the bottom of the pile, treated like animals instead of human beings. As I listened to these victims of pornography, I heard young women describe how they felt about . . . the way women's genitals and breasts are displayed and women's bodies are shown in compromising postures. I thought about the time of slavery, when Black women had their bodies invaded, their teeth and limbs examined, their bodies checked out for breeding, checked out as you would an animal, and I said to myself, "We've come a long way, haven't we?"
>
> Today we have an industry . . . showing women in the same kind of submissive and animalistic roles.

U.S. culture is now severely contaminated by pornography. People actually see differently. Pornography has to become increasingly extreme before people are disturbed by, or even notice, the violence and degradation portrayed in it. Furthermore, very few seem to see the real abuse that is happening to women in the industry. As Zillmann (1985) has shown, "heavy consumption of common forms of pornography fosters an appetite for stronger materials" (p. 127). What was considered hard-core in the past has become soft-core in the present. When will all this end? Will we as a culture forever refuse to read the writing on the wall?

It is women who must demand an end to pornography. The civil rights movement would never have gotten very far if people of color had not mobilized against racism. Many antiracist activists had to be willing to engage in militant actions and to risk suffering grievous consequences—physically, economically, and psychologically. It is imperative that women recognize the need for us to mobilize on this issue. The deep divisions between feminists with regard to pornography, and the unwillingness of most anti-pornography feminists to engage in militant action against it, may be the most serious problem in our efforts to combat this woman-hating propaganda.

The first step in mobilizing more feminists and other women against pornography is to educate them regarding its contents. I wrote *Against Pornography* and have revised and expanded it into *Dangerous Relationships* in the hope that these books will turn large numbers of women from uninformed victims of pornography to informed, committed, risk-taking activists against it.

This is not a call for censorship as the defenders of porn try to make it appear. It is a simple demand for equality. Pornography, like sexual harassment, discriminates against women. Although pornography is harmful to men and to society at large, women and children are its primary victims.

While child pornography is illegal,[6] the laws against adult pornography are totally inadequate; they are also misrepresented by the old-fashioned conception of obscenity; and they are poorly implemented. Rejecting the notion of obscenity, Catharine MacKinnon and Andrea Dworkin (1988) have pointed out that pornography is a civil rights issue. Women have a right not to be targeted by a medium that causes irreparable harm to them.

I have no doubt that if most pornography consisted of pictures of gangs of women raping men, sticking broomsticks up their rectums as the men smile and ejaculate and say, "Encore," or pictures of men holding their male victims down and forcing anal and oral sex on them as women watch and applaud, or women snipping their testicles off with pliers, or women sticking wire up their penile openings, then men would have put a stop to pornography long ago. The fact that pictures like these are acceptable when it is women who are being degraded, but not men, demonstrates yet again that gender discrimination is intrinsic to pornography. Women must unite to fight this form of discrimination against women with all the strength, intelligence, and outrage with which we have fought against many others.

## NOTES

1. This perspective is explained in Russell (1993a, p. 18).

2. National Organization for Women. (1973). *General Resolution on Prostitution.* Unpublished document. (Request from Robert Brannon, PhD, Director, Center for Sex Role Research, Department of Psychology, Brooklyn College City University, Brooklyn, NY)

Because many prostitutes favor decriminalization, well-meaning progressive people often assume that they should therefore endorse this policy. Obviously, those engaged in illegal behavior are likely to prefer it to be made legal, and those employed in a particular job cannot be expected to argue for its demise, even if the job is destructive to them. Hence, the fact that many prostitutes advocate decriminalization does not mean it is the best policy for them or for society.

Prostitution is an institution that exploits women, many of whom have already been severely sexually victimized in childhood. The notion that societies need this institution presumes that men's desires for sexual services, no matter how debased, destructive, or dangerous, must be satisfied. Merely seeking to rehabilitate and relabel the social identity of prostitutes (as "sex workers," for example) is not what is needed.

I believe that prostitution should remain illegal and that the customers and pimps should be incarcerated for sexual exploitation. The widespread practice of punishing the victims, instead of those who victimize them, is blatantly sexist. It reflects the fact that it is largely men who make laws to suit their interests. Since the majority of prostitutes—possibly all of them—are forced or driven into this role by poverty, drug addiction, entrapment by pimps, and/or being trapped in a history of incestuous abuse and/or other kinds of physical or emotional violence, arrest and incarceration are cruel and inappropriate ways to treat them.

3. Even the 1985 Attorney General's Commission on Pornography was unable to get its *Final Report* published by a mainstream publishing house for a considerable time (it was first published by Rutledge Hill Press in Tennessee).

4. Although the Gallup survey was based on telephone interviews and the National Opinion Research Center conducted personal interviews, there is no consensus among researchers on which of these methods is more effective at obtaining honest answers and maximum disclosure. Therefore, the impact of this methodological difference will not be further examined here.

5. Steve Johnson, a representative of this PR firm, Gray and Company, advised the Media Coalition that "a successful effort to relieve publishers, distributors and retailers from harassment will involve communicating several broad themes with which most Americans agree" (*sic*) (a copy of Johnson's letter, dated June 5, 1986, was sent to me by Catherine MacKinnon on July 27, 1986). One of these was that: "*There is no factual or scientific basis for the exaggerated and unfounded allegations that sexually oriented content in contemporary media is in any way a cause of violent or criminal behavior*" (emphasis added).

6. This is not to say that the laws against child pornography are adequately implemented. For example, large quantities of child porn are available on the Internet (see Rimm, 1995).

# APPENDIX 1

## DIRECTORIES' DISPARATE PORNOGRAPHY MAGAZINE SUBSCRIPTION RATES

**Table A.1.1** 1997 Subscription Rates for Selected Pornography Magazines by Source

| | *Source* | | | | |
|---|---|---|---|---|---|
| *Magazine* | *Working Press of the Nation* | *Ulrich's International Periodicals* | *Bacon's Magazine Directory* | *Totals* | *Average* |
| Playboy | 3,400,000 | 3,400,000 | 3,555,663 | 10,355,663 | 3,451,888 |
| Penthouse | 1,300,000 | 1,304,709 | 1,500,000 | 2,804,709 | 1,368,236 |
| Hustler | 500,000 | 500,000 | 1,426,000 | 2,426,000 | 808,667 |
| Club | 700,000 | — | — | 700,000 | 700,000 |
| Gallery | 500,000 | 400,000 | 400,000 | 1,300,000 | 433,333 |
| Oui | 395,000 | — | 320,000 | 715,000 | 357,500 |
| Chic | 100,000 | — | 90,876 | 190,876 | 95,438 |

# APPENDIX 2

## PUBLIC OPINION POLLS ON PORNOGRAPHY

## IS PORNOGRAPHY HARMFUL?

### 1. *Some Negative Effects of Pornography*

*Newsweek Poll: Mixed Feelings on Pornography, March 6, 1985*

This public opinion poll conducted by Gallup was based on a national sample of 1,020 adults interviewed on the telephone (Table A.2.1).

**TABLE A.2.1** Some Negative Effects of Pornography[a, 1]

Thinking of explicit sexual magazines, movies and books, tell me if you believe the following are true or not.

| | *True (%)* | *Not True (%)* | *Don't Know/ No Opinion (%)* |
|---|---|---|---|
| They lead some people to commit rape or sexual violence | 73 | 22 | 5 |
| They lead some people to lose respect for women | 76 | 20 | 4 |
| They lead to a breakdown of public morals | 67 | 29 | 4 |

SOURCE: Gallup poll titled "Mixed Feelings on Pornography," Press et al., 1985, p. 60.
NOTE: a. This table is constructed from data provided in the source.

## 2. *Pornography and Harm to Children*

### *National Family Values, September 11, 1993*[2]

This public opinion poll conducted by Voter/Consumer Research was based on a national sample of 1,100 adults interviewed on the telephone (Table A.2.2).

> Now I'm going to read you a number of statements on social issues. For each of the following statements, please tell me whether you strongly agree, somewhat agree, somewhat disagree, or strongly disagree with that statement. Children are harmed by the presence of sexually explicit materials and adult entertainment in our society.

**TABLE A.2.2** Children Harmed by Pornography in Society

| | *Percentage* |
|---|---|
| Strongly agree | 64 |
| Somewhat agree | 20 |
| Somewhat disagree | 5 |
| Strongly disagree | 7 |
| Neutral/Don't know | 3 |
| Total | 99 |

SOURCE: *Roper Center for Public Opinion Research.* (1996). Question ID: USVCR. 93FAMV R009 [On-Line] From: DIALOG (R) File: 468: Public Opinion

## 3. *Pornography, Rape, and a Breakdown of Morals*

### *General Social Survey, February 5, 1993, and January 27, 1994*

These public opinion polls conducted by the National Opinion Research Center (NORC) were based on personal interviews with two national samples of 2,992 and 1,606 adults, respectively (Tables A.2.3a and b).

> The next questions are about pornography—books, movies, magazines, and photographs that show or describe sex activities. I'm going to read some opinions about the effects of looking at or reading such sexual materials. As I read each

one, please tell me if you think sexual materials do or do not have that effect. a) Sexual materials lead people to commit rape; and b) Sexual materials lead to a breakdown of morals.

**TABLE A.2.3a** Pornography, Rape, and a Breakdown of Morals: Comparison of Two National Samples

a. Sexual materials lead people to commit rape.

| | *1993 (%)* | *1994 (%)* |
|---|---|---|
| Yes | 57 | 48 |
| No | 34 | 42 |
| Don't know | 10 | 10 |
| Total | 101 | 100 |

b. Sexual materials lead to a breakdown of morals.

| | *1993 (%)* | *1994 (%)* |
|---|---|---|
| Yes | 64 | 57 |
| No | 30 | 36 |
| Don't know | 6 | 7 |
| Total | 100 | 100 |

SOURCE: *Roper Center for Public Opinion Research.* (1996). Question ID: USNORC.GSS93 R220C [On-Line] From: DIALOG (R) File: 468: Public Opinion

**TABLE A.2.3b** Pornography, Rape, and a Breakdown of Morals: Opinions of Specific Populations Compared

Percentages of specific populations that believe sexual materials
a. lead people to commit rape; and b. lead to a breakdown of morals.

| | *Commit Rape* | | *Breakdown of Morals* | |
|---|---|---|---|---|
| *Specific Populations* | *1993* | *1994* | *1993* | *1994* |
| *Gender* | | | | |
| Women | 62 | 55 | 69 | 64 |
| Men | 50 | 40 | 57 | 49 |
| *Ethnicity* | | | | |
| White | 57 | 48 | 65 | 58 |
| African American | 58 | 46 | 58 | 49 |

**TABLE A.2.3b** Continued

Percentages of specific populations that believe sexual materials
a. lead people to commit rape; and b. lead to a breakdown of morals.

| | *Commit Rape* | | *Breakdown of Morals* | |
|---|---|---|---|---|
| *Specific Populations* | *1993* | *1994* | *1993* | *1994* |
| *Age in Years* | | | | |
| 18-29 | 54 | 40 | 55 | 48 |
| 30-39 | 44 | 40 | 53 | 49 |
| 40-49 | 45 | 45 | 56 | 53 |
| 50-59 | 68 | 51 | 75 | 62 |
| 60-69 | 73 | 66 | 83 | 74 |
| 70 and over | 81 | 65 | 85 | 74 |
| *Education* | | | | |
| < High school grad | 69 | 61 | 75 | 64 |
| High school grad | 62 | 55 | 65 | 62 |
| Some college | 57 | 41 | 64 | 51 |
| College grad | 44 | 37 | 60 | 47 |
| Postgraduate | 39 | 39 | 47 | 55 |
| *Income ($)* | | | | |
| < 15,000 | 71 | 58 | 72 | 62 |
| 15,000-19,999 | 57 | 58 | 67 | 62 |
| 20,000-29,999 | 61 | 45 | 69 | 50 |
| 30,000-49,999 | 50 | 47 | 56 | 59 |
| 50,000-74,999 | 53 | 41 | 61 | 53 |
| 75,000 and over | 41 | 34 | 54 | 49 |
| *Religion* | | | | |
| Protestant | 62 | 53 | 69 | 63 |
| Catholic | 56 | 45 | 64 | 55 |
| Jewish | 40 | 28 | 60 | 33 |
| None | 36 | 30 | 41 | 30 |
| *Political Affiliation* | | | | |
| Republican | 64 | 56 | 71 | 68 |
| Democrat | 55 | 48 | 61 | 58 |
| Independent | 54 | — | 62 | — |
| *Political Ideology* | | | | |
| Liberal | 40 | 37 | 51 | 41 |
| Moderate | 62 | 51 | 67 | 58 |
| Conservative | 65 | 54 | 71 | 67 |

SOURCE: *Roper Center for Public Opinion Research.* (1996). Question ID: USNORC. GSS94 Q221B [On-Line] From: DIALOG (R) File: 468: Public Opinion

## 4. *The Effects of Nude Magazines and X-Rated Movies*

*People, the Press & Politics: New Political Landscape, reported in the* Times Mirror, *July 13, 1994*

This public opinion poll conducted by Princeton Survey Research Associates (PSRA) was based on telephone interviews with a national sample of 1,009 adults (Table A.2.4).

> Please tell me how much you agree or disagree with each of the following statements. Nude magazines and X-rated movies provide harmless entertainment for those who enjoy it.

**TABLE A.2.4** Nude Magazines and X-Rated Movies Harmless

| *Answers* | *Percentage* |
|---|---|
| Completely agree | 15 |
| Mostly agree | 29 |
| Mostly disagree | 25 |
| Completely disagree | 29 |
| Don't know | 2 |
| Total | 100 |

SOURCE: *Roper Center for Public Opinion Research.* (1996). Question ID: USPSRA.94 JL13 R52G [On-Line] From: DIALOG (R) File: 468: Public Opinion

## 5. *Concern About the Availability of Porn on the Internet*

Newsweek, *February 16, 1995*

This public opinion poll conducted by Princeton Survey Research Associates was based on telephone interviews with a national sample of 752 adults (Table A.2.5).

> How concerned are you about each of the following happening through the *Internet* that links computer users worldwide? How concerned are you about . . . *pornography* being too available to young people . . . very concerned, somewhat concerned, not too concerned or not at all concerned?

**TABLE A.2.5** Degree of Concern That Internet Pornography Is Too Available to Young People

| *Answer* | *Percentage* |
|---|---|
| Very | 67 |
| Somewhat | 18 |
| Not too | 6 |
| Not at all | 7 |
| Don't know | 2 |
| Total | 100 |

SOURCE: *Roper Center for Public Opinion Research.* (1996). Question ID: USPSRNEW.95 FB16 R17A [On-Line] From: DIALOG (R) File: 468: Public Opinion

## 6. *Those Most Concerned About the Availability of Porn on the Internet*

*Newsweek, February 16, 1995*

This public opinion poll conducted by Princeton Survey Research Associates was based on telephone interviews with a national sample of 752 adults (Table A.2.6). (See question in 5 above.)

> How concerned are you about each of the following happening through the Internet that links computer users worldwide? How concerned are you about . . . pornography being too available to young people . . . very concerned, somewhat concerned, not too concerned or not at all concerned?

**TABLE A.2.6** Percentages of Specific Populations That Are Very Concerned That Internet Pornography Is Too Available to Young People

| | *Percentages of Specific Populations That Are "Very Concerned"* |
|---|---|
| *Specific Populations* | *Percentage* |
| *Gender* | |
| Women | 77 |
| Men | 56 |
| *Ethnicity* | |
| White | 64 |
| African American | 91 |
| Asian American | 62 |

*(continued)*

**TABLE A.2.6** Continued

| | *Percentages of Specific Populations That Are "Very Concerned"* |
|---|---|
| *Specific Populations* | *Percentage* |
| *Age in Years* | |
| 18-29 | 54 |
| 30-39 | 60 |
| 40-49 | 68 |
| 50-59 | 77 |
| 60-69 | 72 |
| 70 and over | 83 |
| *Political Affiliation* | |
| Republican | 67 |
| Democrat | 67 |

SOURCE: *Roper Center for Public Opinion Research.* (1996). Question ID: USPSRNEW.95 FB16 R17A [On-Line] From: DIALOG (R) File: 468: Public Opinion

## DESIRE FOR GREATER LEGAL RESTRICTIONS ON PORNOGRAPHY

### 7. *Type of Legal Restrictions on Porn Advocated*

*"Mixed Feelings on Pornography," reported in* Newsweek, *March 6, 1985*

This public opinion poll conducted by Gallup was based on a national sample of 1,020 adults interviewed on the telephone (Table A.2.7).

> Do you think laws should totally ban any of the following activities in your community, allow them as long as there is no public display—or impose no restrictions at all for adult audiences?

TABLE A.2.7 Opinions re: Need for Legal Restrictions on Pornography[a]

| | *Ban (%)* | *No Restriction (%)* | *Don't Know/No Opinion (%)* |
|---|---|---|---|
| Magazines that show sexual violence | 73 | 6 | 6 |
| Theaters showing movies that depict sexual violence | 68 | 9 | 9 |
| Sale or rental of video cassettes featuring sexual violence | 63 | 13 | 13 |

SOURCE: Gallup poll titled "Mixed Feelings on Pornography," Press et al., 1985, p. 60.
NOTE: a. This table is constructed from data provided in the source.

## 8. *Attitude To Restrictions on the Portrayal of Explicit Sex in Mass Media*

*Eight Nation & The Press Survey, January 6, 1994.*

This public opinion poll conducted by Princeton Survey Research Associates (PSRA) was based on telephone interviews with a national sample of 1,494 adults (Table A.2.8).

> I'd like to ask you a few questions about the news organizations generally, including newspapers, television, radio, and magazines: I am going to read a list of reasons why the government might want to restrict what news organizations can report. As I read each, tell me if you favor or oppose any restrictions of the news for this purpose . . . to restrict portrayals of explicit sex.

TABLE A.2.8 Attitude to Restrictions on the Portrayal of Explicit Sex in the Mass Media

| | *Percentage* |
|---|---|
| Favor | 59 |
| Oppose | 36 |
| Don't know | 5 |
| Total | 100 |

SOURCE: *Roper Center for Public Opinion Research.* (1996). Question ID: USPSRA 031694 R37E [On-Line] From: DIALOG (R) File: 468: Public Opinion

## *9. Need for Stricter Laws to Control Porn in Books and Movies by Demographic Variables*

*NBC News*/Wall Street Journal,
*June 10, 1994*

This public opinion poll conducted by Hart and Teeter Research Companies was based on telephone interviews with a national sample of 1,502 adults (Table A.2.9).

> I would like to read several statements about some social issues facing America. . . . We need stricter laws to control pornography in books and movies. Do you agree strongly, agree somewhat, disagree somewhat, or disagree strongly with this statement?

**TABLE A.2.9** Opinions re: Need for Stricter Laws to Control Pornography in Books and Movies by Demographic Variables

| | *Strongly Agree (%)* | *Somewhat Agree (%)* | *Somewhat/Strongly Disagree (%)* |
|---|---|---|---|
| All respondents[a] | 55 | 22 | 21 |
| *Gender* | | | |
| Females | 68 | 17 | 13 |
| Males | 41 | 28 | 30 |
| *Ethnicity* | | | |
| White | 52 | 23 | 23 |
| African American | 69 | 19 | 11 |
| Hispanic | 62 | 21 | 14 |
| Asian American | 58 | 28 | 13 |

**TABLE A.2.9** Continued

| | *Strongly Agree (%)* | *Somewhat Agree (%)* | *Somewhat/Strongly Disagree (%)* |
|---|---|---|---|
| *Age in Years* | | | |
| 18-29 | 47 | 29 | 24 |
| 30-39 | 48 | 23 | 29 |
| 40-49 | 53 | 25 | 19 |
| 50-59 | 61 | 18 | 19 |
| 60 and over | 68 | 16 | 14 |
| *Education* | | | |
| < High school graduate | 74 | 13 | 11 |
| High school graduate | 64 | 20 | 13 |
| Some college | 53 | 22 | 22 |
| College graduate | 41 | 27 | 32 |
| Postgraduate | 39 | 28 | 32 |
| *Income ($)* | | | |
| < 10,000 | 72 | 15 | 10 |
| 10,000-19,999 | 58 | 21 | 20 |
| 20,000-29,999 | 63 | 19 | 16 |
| 30,000-49,999 | 50 | 25 | 23 |
| 50,000-74,999 | 46 | 26 | 27 |
| 75,000 and over | 40 | 26 | 31 |
| *Political Affiliation* | | | |
| Republican | 52 | 22 | 23 |
| Democrat | 59 | 20 | 20 |
| *Political Ideology* | | | |
| Liberal | 45 | 24 | 30 |
| Moderate | 60 | 23 | 16 |
| Conservative | 56 | 23 | 20 |

SOURCE: *Roper Center for Public Opinion Research*. (1996). Question ID: USNBCWSJ. 061794 R12A09 [On-Line] From: DIALOG (R) File: 468: Public Opinion

NOTE: a. The "Don't Know/No Information" category has been omitted. Therefore the row percentages will be very slightly short of 100%.

## 10. *The Desirability of Making Porn on the Internet Illegal*

*Technology and Online Use Survey, May 25, 1995*

This public opinion poll conducted by Princeton Survey Research Associates was based on telephone interviews with a national sample of 3,603 adults (Table A.2.10).

**TABLE A.2.10** Attitude to Pornography on the Internet Being Made Illegal

| | *Favor (%)* | *Oppose (%)* | *Don't Know/ Refused (%)* |
|---|---|---|---|
| Would you favor or oppose a law that would make it illegal for a computer network to carry pornographic or adult material? | 52 | 41 | 7 |

SOURCE: *Roper Center for Public Opinion Research.* (1996). Question ID: USPSRA. 101695 R030 [On-Line] From: DIALOG (R) File: 468: Public Opinion

## NOTES

1. This and other table headings in Appendix 2 have been adapted from the original headings.
2. This date is the first day on which the public opinion poll was conducted. This is also the case for all the other tables accessed on the Internet.

# APPENDIX 3

## FEMINIST ANTI-PORNOGRAPHY EDUCATION AND ACTIVIST LIST

*Compiled by Jan Woodcock*

This list is undoubtedly incomplete. Please send the names of any other feminist anti-porn organizations, resource people, and/or World Wide Web home pages that should be included in a future edition of this book to:

Russell Publications
2018 Shattuck Avenue, #118
Berkeley, California 94704

### Eastern United States

Richard Procida
3850 Tanlan N.W. #104
Washington, D.C. 20007
(Richard does educational slide presentations on porn and gives talks to classes, churches, etc.)

Women Against Pornography (W.A.P.)
P.O. Box 845
Times Square Post Office
New York, New York 10108-0845

## Canada and Midwestern United States

International Networks
P.O. Box 1068
Mt. Pleasant, Michigan 48804-1068
(Jan Woodcock does educational slide presentations on porn and gives talks to audiences, large and small.)

Men Stopping Rape, Inc.
Madison, Wisconsin 53715
(Call [608] 257-4444)

Montreal Men Against Sexism
913 de Bienville
Montreal, Quebec, Canada H2J IV2
(Current organizer: Martin Dufresne; small group of men who give talks and do actions.)

Pornography Awareness
P.O. Box 50269
Kalamazoo, Michigan 49005-0269
(Contact: Annie Macombs, email: anderson@kzoo.edu)

Women's Resource Center
1200 Academy Street
Kalamazoo College
Kalamazoo, Michigan 49006
(Contact: Amy Elman, Ph.D.)

## Northwestern United States

Council for Prostitution Alternatives (C.P.A.)
710 S.E. Grand Avenue, Suite 8
Portland, Oregon 97214

Sexual Exploitation Education Project (S.E.E.P.)
1811 N.E. 39th Avenue
Portland, Oregon 97212
(Active porn education and action group.)

## Mexico and Southwestern United States

Always Causing Legal Unrest (A.C.L.U.)
P.O. Box 2085
Rancho Cordova, California, 95741-2085

Centro de Orientacion y Apoyo a la Mujer
6 a. Rayon y Victoria #99
Apdo. Postal 1133, Suc. "A,"
H. Matamoros, Tam. Mexico

Media Watch
P.O. Box 618
Santa Cruz, California 95061

Wendy Stock, Ph.D.
1306 Bay View Place
Berkeley, California 94708-1802
(Wendy does educational slide presentations on porn and gives talks to audiences large and small.)

## Anti-Pornography Home Pages on the World Wide Web

Nikki Craft — email address: yappie@talkintrash.com

http://www.igc.apc.org/womensnet/dworkin/

http://www.igc.apc.org/nemesis/ACLU/Porn/

http://www.igc.apc.org/nemesis/ACLU/Nikki/

http://www.igc.apc.org/nemesis/ACLU/NudistHallofShame/

http://www.igc.apc.org/nemesis/ACLU/SportsHallofShame/

Diana E. H. Russell
http://www.mills.edu/ACAD_INFO/emeritus_russell.html

Linnea Smith's *Playboy* and *Sports Illustrated* site
http://www.talkintrash.com

The Women's Network of the Red River Valley
(a feminist Web site opposed to pornography)
http://rrnet.com/wnrrv

# REFERENCES

Abel, Gene, David Barlow, Edward Blanchard, & Donald Guild. (1977). The components of rapists' sexual arousal. *Archives of General Psychiatry, 34,* 895-903.

Abel, Gene, Mary Mittelman, & Judith Becker. (1985). Sexual offenders: Results of assessment and recommendations for treatment. In Mark Ben-Aron, Stephen Hucker, & Christopher Webster (Eds.), *Clinical criminology: The assessment and treatment of criminal behavior* (pp. 191-205). Toronto: University of Toronto, Clarke Institute of Psychiatry.

*Attorney General's Commission on Pornography: Final report.* (1986). Nashville, TN: Rutledge Hill Press.

Bacon's Information Inc. (Annual). *Bacon's magazine directory.* Chicago: Author.

Baron, Larry, & Murray Straus. (1984). Sexual stratification, pornography, and rape in the United States. In Neil Malamuth & Edward Donnerstein (Eds.), *Pornography and sexual aggression* (pp. 185-209). New York: Academic Press.

Bem, Sandra. (1991). Gender schema theory: A cognitive account of sex typing. *Psychological Review, 88,* 354-364.

Beneke, Timothy. (1982). *Men on rape.* New York: St. Martin's.

Bianchi, Alessandra. (1996). What's love got to do with it? *Inc., 18*(6), 76-85.

Bogdanovich, Peter. (1984). *The killing of the unicorn: Dorothy Stratten 1960-1980.* New York: William Morrow.

Briere, John, Shawn Corne, Marsha Runtz, & Neil Malamuth. (1984). *The rape arousal inventory: Predicting actual and potential sexual aggression in a university population.* Paper presented at the American Psychological Association Meeting, Toronto.

Briere, John, & Neil Malamuth. (1983). Self-reported likelihood of sexually aggressive behavior: Attitudinal versus sexual explanations. *Journal of Research in Personality, 17,* 315-323.

Briere, John, Neil Malamuth, & James Check. (1985). Sexuality and rape-supportive beliefs. *International Journal of Women's Studies, 8,* 398-403.

Brownmiller, Susan. (1975). *Against our will: Men, women and rape.* New York: Simon & Schuster.

Bryant, Jennings. (1985). Unpublished transcript of testimony to the Attorney General's Commission on Pornography Hearings, Houston, TX, 128-157. (Request for information can be made to Department of Justice, Tenth Street and Constitution Avenue, NW, Washington, DC 20530; phone: 202-514-2000)

Burt, Martha. (1980). Cultural myths and supports for rape. *Journal of Personality and Social Psychology, 38*(2), 217-230.

Check, James. (1985). *The effects of violent and non-violent pornography.* Ottawa: Department of Justice, Canada.

Check, James. (1995). Teenage training: The effects of pornography on adolescent males. In Laura Lederer & Richard Delgado (Eds.), *The price we pay: The case against racist speech, hate propaganda, and pornography* (pp. 89-91). New York: Hill and Wang.

Check, James, & Ted Guloien. (1989). Reported proclivity for coercive sex following repeated exposure to sexually violent pornography, non-violent dehumanizing pornography, and erotica. In Dolf Zillmann & Jennings Bryant (Eds.), *Pornography: Recent research, interpretations, and policy considerations* (pp. 159-184). Hillsdale, NJ: Lawrence Erlbaum.

Check, James, & Neil Malamuth. (1985). An empirical assessment of some feminist hypotheses about rape. *International Journal of Women's Studies, 8,* 414-423.

Check, James, & Kristin Maxwell. (1992, June). *Children's consumption of pornography and their attitudes regarding sexual violence.* Paper presented at the Canadian Psychological Association Meetings, Quebec.

Cline, Victor. (Ed.). (1974). *Where do you draw the line?* Provo, UT: Brigham Young University Press.

Coomaraswamy, Radhika. (1997, February 24). *United Nations report on the mission of the Special Rapporteur to South Africa on the issue of rape in the community.* Geneva, Switzerland: United Nations, Economic and Social Council.

Cowan, Gloria, & Robin Campbell. (1994). Racism and sexism in interracial pornography: A content analysis. *Psychology of Women Quarterly, 18,* 323-338.

Cowan, Gloria, Carole Lee, Daniella Levy, & Debra Snyder. (1988). Dominance and inequality in X-rated videocassettes. *Psychology of Women Quarterly, 12,* 299-311.

Cowan, Gloria, & Wendy Stock. (1995). The costs of denial: Self-censorship of research on degrading/dehumanizing pornography. In Laura Lederer & Richard Delgado

(Eds.), *The price we pay: The case against racist speech, hate propaganda, and pornography* (pp. 104-108). New York: Hill and Wang.

Dietz, Park Elliot, & Alan Sears. (1987/1988). Pornography and obscenity sold in "adult bookstores": A survey of 5132 books, magazines, and films in four American cities. *Journal of Law Reform, 21*(1 & 2), 7-46.

Donnerstein, Edward. (1983). Unpublished transcript of testimony to the Public Hearings on Ordinances to Add Pornography as Discrimination against Women. Committee on Government Operations, City Council, Minneapolis, MN, 4-12.

Donnerstein, Edward. (1984). Pornography: Its effects on violence against women. In Neil Malamuth & Edward Donnerstein (Eds.), *Pornography and sexual aggression* (pp. 53-84). New York: Academic Press.

Donnerstein, Edward. (1985). Unpublished transcript of testimony to the Attorney General's Commission on Pornography Hearings, Houston, TX, 5-33. (Request for information can be made to Department of Justice, Tenth Street and Constitution Avenue, NW, Washington, DC 20530; phone: 202-514-2000)

Donnerstein, Edward, & Daniel Linz. (1985). Presentation paper to the Attorney General's Commission on Pornography, Houston, TX.

Donnerstein, Edward, Daniel Linz, & Steven Penrod. (1987). *The question of pornography: Research findings and policy implications.* New York: Free Press.

Dworkin, Andrea. (1988). *Letters From a War Zone.* New York: Dutton.

Dworkin, Andrea, & Catherine MacKinnon. (1988). *Pornography and civil rights.* Minneapolis, MN: Organizing Against Pornography.

Einsiedel, Edna. (1986). *Social science report.* Paper prepared for the Attorney General's Commission on Pornography, Department of Justice, Washington, DC.

Endicott, R. Crag. (1996, June 17). Ad age 300: The annual countdown. *Advertising Age 1996, 67*(25).

Everywoman. (1988). *Pornography and sexual violence: Evidence of the links.* London: Everywoman.

Finkelhor, David. (1984). *Child sexual abuse: New theory and research.* New York: Free Press.

Fishman, Stephen. (1996). *Copyright handbook: How to protect and use written works.* Berkeley, CA: Nolo Press.

Frost, Richard, & John Stauffer. (1987). The effects of social class, gender, and personality on physiological responses to filmed violence. *Journal of Communication, 37*(2), 29-45.

Goldstein, Michael, & Harold Kant. (1973). *Pornography and sexual deviance.* Berkeley: University of California Press.

Goodchilds, Jacqueline, & Gail Zellman. (1984). Sexual signalling and sexual aggression in adolescent relationships. In Neil Malamuth & Edward Donnerstein (Eds.), *Pornography and sexual aggression* (pp. 233-246). New York: Academic Press.

Hite, Shere. (1981). *The Hite report on male sexuality.* New York: Knopf.

Holt, Patricia. (1994, September 4). Pornography: See if you object. *San Francisco Chronicle,* Book Review, p. 2.

Itzin, Catherine. (Ed.). (1992). *Pornography: Women, violence and civil liberties.* New York: Oxford University Press.

Itzin, Catherine. (1996). Pornography and the organisation of child sexual abuse. In Peter Bibby (Ed.), *Organized abuse: The current debate* (pp. 167-196). Aldershot, UK: Arena.

Koss, Mary P., & Thomas Dinero. (1988). Predictors of sexual aggression among a national sample of male college students. In Vernon Quinsey & Robert Prentky (Eds.), *Human sexual aggression: Current perspectives* [Special issue]. *Annals of the New York Academy of Sciences, 528,* 133-147.

Koss, Mary P., Christine Gidycz, & Nadine Wisniewski. (1987). The scope of rape: Incidence and prevalence of sexual aggression and victimization in a national sample of higher education students. *Journal of Consulting and Clinical Psychology, 55,* 162-170.

Lederer, Laura. (Ed.). (1980). *Take back the night: Women on pornography.* New York: William Morrow.

Longino, Helen. (1980). What is pornography? In Laura Lederer (Ed.), *Take back the night: Women on pornography* (pp. 40-54). New York: William Morrow.

Lovelace, Linda. (1981). *Ordeal.* New York: Berkeley Books.

Lovelace, Linda. (1986). *Out of bondage.* Secaucus, NJ: Lyle Stuart.

MacKinnon, Catharine. (1987). *Feminism unmodified: Discourses on life and law.* Cambridge, MA: Harvard University Press.

Madonna. (1992). *Sex.* New York: Warner Books.

Malamuth, Neil. (1981a). Rape fantasies as a function of exposure to violent sexual stimuli. *Archives of Sexual Behavior, 10,* 33-47.

Malamuth, Neil. (1981b). Rape proclivity among males. *Journal of Social Issues, 37*(4), 138-157.

Malamuth, Neil. (1984). Aggression against women: Cultural and individual causes. In Neil Malamuth & Edward Donnerstein (Eds.), *Pornography and sexual aggression* (pp. 19-52). New York: Academic Press.

Malamuth, Neil. (1985). Unpublished transcript of testimony to the Attorney General's Commission on Pornography Hearings, Houston, TX, 68-110. (Request for information can be made to Department of Justice, Tenth Street and Constitution Avenue, NW, Washington, DC 20530; phone: 202-514-2000)

Malamuth, Neil. (1986). *Do sexually violent media indirectly contribute to anti-social behavior?* Unpublished paper prepared for the Surgeon General's Workshop on Pornography and Public Health, Arlington, VA.

Malamuth, Neil. (1989). Sexually violent media, thought patterns, and anti-social behavior. *Public Communication and Behavior, 2,* 159-203.

Malamuth, Neil, & James Check. (1981). The effects of mass media exposure on acceptance of violence against women: A field experiment. *Journal of Research in Personality, 15,* 436-446.

Malamuth, Neil, & James Check. (1985). The effects of aggressive pornography on beliefs in rape myths: Individual differences. *Journal of Research in Personality, 19,* 299-320.

Malamuth, Neil, & Edward Donnerstein. (Eds.). (1984). *Pornography and sexual aggression.* New York: Academic Press.

Malamuth, Neil, Scott Haber, & Seymour Feshbach. (1980). Testing hypotheses regarding rape: Exposure to sexual violence, sex differences, and the "normality" of rapists. *Journal of Research in Personality, 14,* 121-137.

Malamuth, Neil, & Barry Spinner. (1980). A longitudinal content analysis of sexual violence in the best-selling erotic magazines. *Journal of Sex Research, 16*(3), 226-237.

Maxwell, Kristin, & James Check. (1992, June). *Adolescents' rape myth attitudes and acceptance of forced sexual intercourse.* Abstract of paper presented at the Canadian Psychological Association Meetings, Quebec.

Mayall, Alice, & Russell, Diana. (1993). Racism in pornography. In Diana Russell (Ed.), *Making violence sexy: Feminist views on pornography,* pp. 167-177. New York: Teachers College Press.

McKenzie-Mohr, Doug, & Mark Zanna. (1990). Treating women as sexual objects: Look to the (gender schematic) male who has viewed pornography. *Personality and Social Psychology Bulletin, 16*(2), 296-308.

Medea, Andra, & Kathleen Thompson. (1974). *Against rape.* New York: Farrar, Straus & Giroux.

Mosher, Donald. (1971). Sex callousness toward women. *Technical Reports of the Commission on Obscenity and Pornography, 8.* Washington, DC: Government Printing Office.

National Organization for Women. (1973). *General resolution on prostitution.* Unpublished document. (Available from Robert Brannon, PhD, Co-Chair of NOW NYS Task Force on Pornography, at the Center for Sex Role Research, Department of Psychology, Brooklyn College City University, Brooklyn, NY)

National Research Bureau, Inc. (Annual). *Working press of the nation: Magazine and editorial directory* (Vol. 2). Burlington, IA: Author.

Olojede, Dele. (1997, February 1). Tidal wave of rapes alarms South Africa. *San Francisco Chronicle,* p. A13.

Pally, Marcia. (1994). *Sex and sensibility.* Hopewell, NJ: Ecco Press.

Palys, T. S. (1986). Testing the common wisdom: The social content of video pornography. *Canadian Psychology, 27*(1), 22-35.

Parents find violent TV a turnoff. (1996, September 10). *San Francisco Chronicle,* p. A2.

Press, Aric, with Tessa Namuth, Susan Agrest, MacLean Gander, Gerald Lubenow, Michaeal Reese, David Friendly, & Ann McDaniels. (1985, March 18). The war against pornography. *Newsweek,* pp. 58-66.

*Public Hearings on Ordinances to Add Pornography as Discrimination Against Women.* (1983). Committee on Government Operations, City Council, Minneapolis, MN.

Rachman, S., & R. J. Hodgson. (1968). Experimentally-induced "sexual fetishism": Replication and development. *Psychological Record, 18,* 25-27.

Radford, Jill, & Diana E. H. Russell. (Eds.). (1992). *Femicide: The politics of woman killing*. New York: Twayne.

Rimm, Marty. (1995). Marketing pornography on the information superhighway: A survey of 917,410 images, descriptions, short stories and animations downloaded 8.5 million times by consumers in over 2000 cities in forty countries, provinces, and territories. *The Georgetown Law Journal, 83*(5), 1849-1934.

Russell, Diana E. H. (1975). *The politics of rape.* New York: Stein & Day.

Russell, Diana E. H. (1980). Pornography and violence: What does the new research say? In Laura Lederer (Ed.), *Take back the night: Women on pornography* (pp. 218-238). New York: William Morrow.

Russell, Diana E. H. (1984). *Sexual exploitation: Rape, child sexual abuse, and workplace harassment.* Beverly Hills, CA: Sage.

Russell, Diana E. H. (1988). Pornography and rape: A causal model. *Political Psychology, 9*(1), 41-73.

Russell, Diana E. H. (1991). Rape and child sexual abuse in Soweto: An interview with community leader Mary Mabaso. *South African Sociological Review, 3*(2), 62-83.

Russell, Diana E. H. (1993a). The experts cop out. In Diana E. H. Russell (Ed.), *Making violence sexy: Feminist views on pornography.* New York: Teachers College Press.

Russell, Diana E. H. (Ed.). (1993b). *Making violence sexy: Feminist views on pornography.* New York: Teachers College Press.

Russell, Diana E. H. (1994a). *Against pornography: The evidence of harm.* Berkeley, CA: Russell Publications.

Russell, Diana E. H. (1994b). U.S. pornography invades South Africa: A content analysis of *Playboy* and *Penthouse*. In Saras Jagwanth, Pamela-Jane Schwikkasd, & Brenda Grant (Eds.), *Women and the law* (pp. 285-323). Pretoria, South Africa: Human Sciences Research Council Publishers.

Russell, Diana E. H. (1995). Nadine Strossen: The pornography industry's wet dream. *On the Issues, 4*(3), 32-34.

Russell, Diana E. H. (1996a). Patricia Ireland thrown by pornography question. *Media Watch, 3*(1).

Russell, Diana E. H. (1996b). Review of Handelman's documentary film "Bloodsisters." *Media Watch, 3*(1).

Russell, Diana E. H. (1998). Pornography: Towards a non-sexist policy for the new South Africa. *Agenda: A Journal About Women and Gender.*

*S&M: One foot out of the closet.* (1980, May). San Francisco: KQED-TV.

Scott, Joseph, & Steven Cuvelier. (1987). Violence in *Playboy* magazine: A longitudinal content analysis. *Archives of Sexual Behavior, 16,* 279-288.

Scott, Joseph, & Steven Cuvelier. (1993). Violence and sexual violence in pornography: Is it really increasing? *Archives of Sexual Behavior, 22*(4), 357-371.

Scully, Diana. (1985). *The role of violent pornography in justifying rape.* Paper prepared for the Attorney General's Commission on Pornography Hearings, Houston, TX.

Senn, Charlene. (1992, June). *Women's contact with male consumers: One link between pornography and women's experiences of male violence.* Paper presented at the Canadian Psychological Association Meetings, Quebec.

Senn, Charlene. (1993). Women's responses to pornography. In Diana E. H. Russell (Ed.), *Making violence sexy: Feminist views on pornography.* New York: Teachers College Press.

Senn, Charlene, & Lorraine Radtke. (1986, June). *A comparison of women's reactions to violent pornography, non-violent pornography, and erotica.* Paper presented at the Canadian Psychological Association, Toronto.

Silbert, Mimi, & Ayala Pines. (1984). Pornography and sexual abuse of women. *Sex Roles, 10*(11-12), 857-868.

Slade, Joseph. (1984, Summer). Violence in the hard-core pornography film: A historical survey. *Journal of Communication,* pp. 148-163.

Smith, Don. (1976a). *Sexual aggression in American pornography: The stereotype of rape.* Paper presented at the American Sociological Association Meetings, New York City.

Smith, Don. (1976b). The social content of pornography. *Journal of Communication, 26,* 16-33.

Snitow, Ann, Stansell, Christine, & Thompson, Sharon (Eds.). (1983). *Powers of desire: The politics of sexuality.* New York: New Feminist Library.

Sommers, Evelyn, & James Check. (1987). An empirical investigation of the role of pornography in the verbal and physical abuse of women. *Violence and Victims, 2*(3), 189-209.

*The standard periodical directory* (20th ed.). (1996). New York: Oxbridge Communications.

Strossen, Nadine. (1995). *Defending pornography: Free speech, sex, and the fight for women's rights.* New York: Scribner.

Teitelbaum, Richard. (1996, January 15). Why *Penthouse* is in the dog house (Adult magazine sales decline). *Fortune,* p. 20.

Testimony from public hearings on the Ordinance to Add Pornography as Discrimination Against Women. (1993). In Diana E. H. Russell (Ed.), *Making violence sexy: Feminist views on pornography* (pp. 48-62). New York: Teachers College Press.

Theodorson, George, & Achilles Theodorson. (1979). *A modern dictionary of sociology.* New York: Barnes & Noble.

*Ulrich's international periodical directory.* (Annual). Vol. 3. New Providence, NJ: R. R. Bowker.

U.S. Bureau of the Census. (1996). *Statistical abstract of the United States, 1996.* Austin, TX: Hoover's Business Press.

The war against pornography. (1985). *Newsweek.* March 18, pp. 58-66.

White, Van. (1984, September). Pornography and pride. *Essence,* p. 186.

Wilhem, Susan. (1993). Testimony on pornography and marital brutality. In Diana E. H. Russell (Ed.), *Making violence sexy: Feminist views on pornography.* New York: Teachers College Press.

Zillmann, Dolf. (1985). Unpublished transcript of testimony to the Attorney General's Commission on Pornography Hearings, Houston, TX, 110-157. (Request for information can be made to Department of Justice, Tenth Street and Constitution Avenue, NW, Washington, DC 20530; phone: 202-514-2000)

Zillmann, Dolf, & Jennings Bryant. (1984). Effects of massive exposure to pornography. In Neil Malamuth & Edward Donnerstein (Eds.), *Pornography and sexual aggression* (pp. 115-138). New York: Academic Press.

Zillmann, Dolf, & Jennings Bryant. (1989). *Pornography: Recent research, interpretations, and policy considerations.* Hillsdale, NJ: Lawrence Erlbaum.

# INDEX

# ABOUT THE AUTHOR

**Diana E. H. Russell** obtained her B.A. from the University of Cape Town in South Africa in 1958 and a Postgraduate Diploma from the London School of Economics and Political Science (with Distinction) in 1961. She was the recipient of LSE's Mostyn Lloyd Memorial Prize, which is awarded to the best student studying for the Postgraduate Diploma. She subsequently received her Ph.D. from Harvard University in 1970.

She is Professor Emerita of Sociology at Mills College, Oakland, California, where she taught sociology and women's studies for 22 years. She is author, editor, or coeditor of 14 books (see the list at the beginning of this volume). Her book *The Secret Trauma: Incest in the Lives of Girls and Women* won the 1986 C. Wright Mills Award for outstanding social science research that addresses an important social issue.

She has been a politically active feminist since 1969. That year she started teaching the first course in women's studies at Mills College. She was one of the main organizers of the 1976 International Tribunal on Crimes Against Women, and later that year helped to found the first feminist anti-pornography organization in the United States (Women Against Violence in Pornography and Media). She remained active in this organization for many years. In 1996-1997, she helped organize the successful feminist campaign against Milos Forman's heroization of pornographer Larry Flynt in *The People vs. Larry Flynt*.

Russell, who lives in Berkeley, California, has lectured widely, in the United States and abroad, about the political situation in South Africa, rape, incest, child sexual abuse in general, pornography, femicide, and all forms of violence against women. She has been arrested three times for her political activism, in South Africa (1963), in England (1974), and the United States (1990).